ISBN 978-0-259-79852-1
PIBN 10825136

1 MONTH OF
FREE
READING

at

www.ForgottenBooks.com

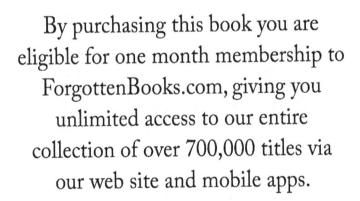

By purchasing this book you are eligible for one month membership to ForgottenBooks.com, giving you unlimited access to our entire collection of over 700,000 titles via our web site and mobile apps.

To claim your free month visit:

www.forgottenbooks.com/free825136

English
Français
Deutsche
Italiano
Español
Português

www.forgottenbooks.com

Mythology Photography **Fiction**
Fishing Christianity **Art** Cooking
Essays Buddhism Freemasonry
Medicine **Biology** Music **Ancient
Egypt** Evolution Carpentry Physics
Dance Geology **Mathematics** Fitness
Shakespeare **Folklore** Yoga Marketing
Confidence Immortality Biographies
Poetry **Psychology** Witchcraft
Electronics Chemistry History **Law**
Accounting **Philosophy** Anthropology
Alchemy Drama Quantum Mechanics
Atheism Sexual Health **Ancient History**
Entrepreneurship Languages Sport
Paleontology Needlework Islam
Metaphysics Investment Archaeology
Parenting Statistics Criminology
Motivational

THE MEMOIRS

OF

MME ELISABETH LOUISE VIGÉE-LE BRUN

1755-1789

MADAME VIGÉE-LE BRUN IN HER STUDIO.
From an anonymous XVIIIth-century engraving.

VIGÉE-LE BRUN, 1755–1789

TRANSLATED BY

GERARD SHELLEY

NEW YORK

GEORGE H. DORAN COMPANY

PUBLISHERS

Printed in Great Britain by
UNWIN BROTHERS, LIMITED, THE GRESHAM PRESS, LONDON AND WOKING

ILLUSTRATIONS

6

A YOUNG ARTIST.

From an anonymous XVIIIth-century drawing in the Musée du Louvre.

To face p. 7.

INTRODUCTION

WOMAN HATH HER VICTORIES no less renowned than man, may be truthfully said of so celebrated a portrait-painter as Madame Vigée-Le Brun. When a man's sayings are heard on the lips of the lowliest dwellers of a country, though he be dead and his name unknown to them, he may be considered to have endowed mankind with a part of himself that is immortal. Madame Vigée-Le Brun achieved this victory in paint. There is hardly a civilized home that is unfamiliar with her portrait of herself and daughter under the title of *La Tendresse Maternelle*. So great a triumph of a woman, coupled with her fame as the favourite portraitist of the unfortunate Queen Marie-Antoinette, and as the fashionable painter of all the aristocracies of Europe, cannot fail to excite one's curiosity concerning her life and personality.

Elisabeth Louise Vigée was born in Paris, in the Rue Coq-Héron, on the 16th April, 1755, the same year in which the Archduchess Marie-Antoinette was born in Vienna. Her father was a pastel painter of considerable talent, who had taken part in the exhibitions of the Academy of Saint Luc since 1751. At an early age she showed signs of having inherited her father's gift, and

7

received from him every encouragement to develop it. In her *Memoirs* she relates her first steps in mastering her art. She was thirteen years old when her father died, and after that event she determined to earn her living by painting. It was not long before she began to make an impression with a few portraits of a serious kind, which suggested a pleasant imitation of Greuze, and persuaded a few persons to give her a commission.

Her good looks and pleasant manner ensured for her a certain social success which was very useful to her in her career as an artist. She received invitations from all quarters and was soon to be found at all the smartest gatherings of Paris, where she was able to observe the grand manners and brilliant conversations, of which she has left so delightful an account in her *Memoirs*.

Her first début as an artist before the public was at the exhibition of the Academy of Saint Luc in August 1774, at the age of nineteen. Her fame grew by leaps and bounds. In 1776 she married M. Le Brun, a painter and dealer in pictures.

In 1779 she painted the portrait of Marie-Antoinette, and from that time her reputation was established throughout Europe. The young Queen conceived a lasting affection for her and gave her every protection. It was owing to the intervention of Marie-Antoinette that Mme Vigée-Le Brun was received into the French Academy without the customary ballot.

The doors of her house in the Rue de Cléry now opened to receive the most distinguished and wittiest people of the age. Her salon became famous throughout Europe. Of the famous people that frequented it, and of the delights that were enjoyed there, she has left us a charming account in her *Memoirs*. The latter are all the more interesting and moving because they portray a brilliant and agreeable society that was amusing itself apparently with no suspicion of the terrible days in store, when so many of the revellers were to lose their heads on the scaffold.

Her meteoric success was not without its darkness. She was cruelly calumniated, especially regarding her relations with a Minister she had painted.

Her passion for painting lasted all her life. At sixty-eight she was able to write : " Painting is always for me a distraction that will only end when I die." Nevertheless, she was able to find another in writing her *Memoirs*. These appeared in three volumes in 1835-37. They took the form of a series of letters addressed to her old friend Princess Kourakin, whose acquaintance she had made during her long sojourn at the Court of the Empress Catherine II in Russia.

Madame Vigée-Le Brun died in Paris on the 29th May, 1842, at the age of eighty-seven, leaving a world grateful both for her paintings and for her lively *Memoirs*.

Although the three volumes of *Memoirs* have previously been translated into English, that section of this book—" Notes and Portraits "—has not previously been translated.

G. S.

JOSEPH VERNET.
From an engraving by Cathelin (1770).

To face p 10.

Memoirs of Mme Elisabeth Louise Vigée-Le Brun

CHAPTER I

My childhood—My parents—I am sent to a convent—My passion for painting—My father's circle—Doyen, Poinsinet, Davesne—I leave the convent—My brother.

MY VERY DEAR FRIEND, you urge me so warmly to write my memoirs for you, that I have decided to satisfy your desire. Imagine what it will mean to my heart to recall the various events I have witnessed and the friends who exist no more save in my thoughts ! Nevertheless, the task will be an easy one, for my heart loves to remember, and in my hours of loneliness those dear departed friends surround me still, so vivid do they appear to my imagination. Moreover, I will add to my story the notes I took at different times of my life on a number of people who sat to me for their portraits and who, for the greater part, belonged to my circle of society. Thanks to this help, the sweetest moments of my life will be made known to you as intimately as I know them myself.

I will take first of all, dear friend, my earliest years, because it was in them that the nature of my future life was foreseen, my love of painting having revealed itself in my childhood. I was sent to a convent at the age of six and remained there till I was eleven. During that time I was always busy with the pencil, drawing whenever and wherever I could. My writing books, and even those of my school-fellows, were filled with marginal drawings of little heads and profiles. On the dormitory walls I would draw faces and landscapes with coloured chalks. As you may suppose, I was often punished. In the intervals of recreation I used to trace in the sand everything that came into my head. I remember drawing by lamp-light, at the age of seven or eight, the portrait of a man with a beard, which I have kept ever since. I showed it to my father, who was delighted and exclaimed : " You will be a painter, my child, if ever there was one."

I mention all this in order to show that my passion for painting was born in me. This passion has never weakened ; in fact, I believe it has done nothing but increase with the passage of time, for even to this day I feel all its charm, which will not cease, I hope, except with my life. Moreover, it is to this divine passion that I owe not only my fortune but my happiness as well, since in my young days, as at the present time, it has brought me into touch with all the most agreeable and distinguished men and women of Europe. The remembrance of so many remarkable persons

I have known often imparts a charm to my solitude. Thereby I still live with those who are no more, and my thanks are due to Providence for having left me this reflection of a bygone happiness.

As my health at the convent was very weak, my father and mother would often come and take me away to stay with them for a few days, a proceeding which charmed me in every respect. My father, whose name was Vigée, was very good at pastel painting ; some of his portraits are worthy of Latour. He painted also in oils in the manner of Watteau. The one you have seen at my house, has an excellent colouring and is ingeniously executed. But, coming back to the pleasures I enjoyed in my childhood's home, I must tell you that my father allowed me to paint several heads in pastels and also to dabble with his crayons all day.

He was so deeply in love with his art that he was often absent-minded. I remember how one day, being dressed for dining out, he left the house, but returned a short while after in order to give a few touches to a picture he had just begun. He took off his wig, put on a nightcap, and went out again with the cap on his head and wearing a gold-laced coat, a sword at his side, etc. Had not a neighbour apprised him of his absent-mindedness, he would have gone all round the town in that costume.

My father had plenty of wit. His natural good spirits infected everybody, and it was on account of his delightful conversation that people came to have their portraits painted by him. Perhaps you already know the following anecdote? One day, being at work on the portrait of a rather pretty woman, he noticed that when he was doing her mouth she incessantly twisted it up in order to make it smaller. Losing patience with this way of going on, my father said to her very coolly: "Don't put yourself out like that, Madam. If you wish, I will paint you with no mouth at all."

My mother was very beautiful. This fact is brought out in the pastel portrait of her which my father made, and in the oil painting which I made later. Her character was austere. My father adored her like a divinity ; but low females swept him off his feet. New Year's Day was a feast day for him : he would walk about all Paris without paying a single visit, merely to embrace all the girls he met under the pretext of wishing them a happy New Year.

My mother was very pious. I, too, was pious at heart. We used always to hear High Mass and attend the services of the Church. During Lent especially we never missed any, not even the evening prayers. I have always been fond of religious music, while at that time the sound of the organ used to make such an impression on me that I could not help shedding tears. Now the sound of the organ always reminds me of my father's loss.

At that period, my father was in the habit of gathering together in the evening several artists

14

and men of letters. Foremost among these was Doyen, the painter of historical subjects. He was my father's intimate companion and my first friend. (Doyen was the best man in the world, full of wit and sagacity. His appreciations of men and things were always perfectly true. Moreover, he used to speak about painting with so much warmth that he made my heart beat.) Another celebrity was Poinsinet, who was very witty and gay. Perhaps you have heard talk of his amazing credulity. It was continually laying him open to the weirdest mystifications. One day, for instance, he allowed himself to be persuaded that there existed the office of Fire-screener to the King. Accordingly, he was placed before a fire fierce enough to roast his calves. However much he desired to get away from the heat, he was told : " Don't stir ! You must get accustomed to the great heat, otherwise you will not get the office l " Nevertheless, Poinsinet was far from being a fool. Several of his works are still admired nowadays, and he was the first man of letters to obtain three dramatic successes the same evening : *Ernelide,* at the Grand Opéra ; *Le Cercle,* at the Théâtre Français ; and *Tom Jones,* at the Opéra Comique. Someone said regarding *Le Cercle,* in which the society of that period is so well portrayed, that Poinsinet must have eavesdropped at the doors. Poinsinet's end was most tragic. Somebody gave him the taste for travel. He started with Spain and perished in crossing the Guadalquivir.

I must mention a man called Davesne, painter and poet, who was rather mediocre in both these arts, but whose very witty conversation secured for him the privilege of being admitted to my father's evenings. Here is a sample of his verses, which I have somehow always remembered and which, I believe, have never been printed :

> Plus n'est le temps, où de mes seuls couplets
> Ma Lise aimait à se voir célébrée ;
> Plus n'est le temps où de mes seuls bouquets
> Je la voyais toujours parée.
> Les vers que l'amour me dictait
> Ne répétaient que le nom de Lisette,
> Et Lisette les écoutait.
> Plus d'un baiser payait ma chansonette ;
> Au même prix qui n'eût été poète ? [1]

Although I was little more than a child at the time, I remember quite well how merry these suppers of my father were. I was made to leave the table before the dessert, but from my bedroom I could hear the laughter, the mirth, and the songs, of which I couldn't understand a word, it is true, but which, for all that, made my holidays a time of delight.

At the age of eleven I left the convent for good, after having made my first Communion. Davesne, who painted in oils, asked to be allowed to teach me how to use the palette. His wife

---

[1] " Gone are the days when my Lise loved to see herself celebrated in my verse alone. Gone are the days when I saw her adorned with my nosegays alone. The verses dictated to me by Love knew no other name but Lisette, and Lisette listened to them. Many a kiss was my song's reward. Who would not have been a poet at the same price ? "

would take me to his house. They were so poor that they filled me with sadness and pity. One day, as I wished to finish painting a head I had started, they made me stay to dinner with them. It consisted of soup and some baked apples. I think they never got a regular meal except when they had supper at my father's.

I was immensely happy in not leaving my parents any more. My brother, who was three years younger than myself, was as beautiful as an angel. His intelligence was far beyond his age. He was so successful in his studies that he always returned from school with the most flattering reports. I was far from having his vivacity, wit, and above all, his handsome face; for at that period of my life I was ugly. I had an enormous forehead and deep-set eyes; my nose was the only pretty feature of my pale, thin face. Besides, I had grown so rapidly that I found it impossible to keep upright; I bent like a reed. These deficiencies grieved my mother. Indeed, I fancied she had a weakness for my brother, for she pampered him and readily forgave him his youthful shortcomings, whereas she was very severe with me. On the other hand, my father loaded me with kindness and indulgence. His tenderness endeared him more and more to my heart, so much so that he is always before my mind, and I do not think I have forgotten one word of what he said in my presence. How often did I recall in 1789 the following trait as though it were a sort of prophecy! One day, as my father was coming away from a dinner of the Intellectuals, at which Diderot, Helvétius, and d'Alembert were present, he seemed so sad that my mother asked him what was the matter. " All what I've just heard, my dear friend," he replied, " makes me think that the world will soon be upside down."

CATHERINE II, EMPRESS OF RUSSIA.
Drawn by G. Rotari.

To face p 19

CHAPTER II

HITHERTO, MY DEAR FRIEND, I have
told you of my joys alone ; I must now
tell you of the first affliction which my
heart suffered, the first sorrow I experienced.

I had just spent a year of happiness in my
parents' house, when my father fell ill. He had
swallowed a fish-bone, which lodged in his stomach
and necessitated several incisions in order to ex-
tract it. The operations were carried out by the
cleverest surgeon of the time, a Brother Côme,
in whom we had the fullest confidence, and who
looked like a saint. Notwithstanding the great
devotion with which he looked after my father,
the wounds festered, and at the end of two months'
suffering my father's condition left no hope of
recovery. My mother wept day and night. As
for myself, I will not attempt to describe my
desolation : I was about to lose the best of fathers,
my support, my guide, the one whose indulgence
encouraged my first attempts !

When he realized his end was approaching, my father sent for my brother and me. We went up to the bed, sobbing. His face was terribly altered ; his eyes and facial expression, which had always been so lively, showed no longer any movement. The paleness and chill of death had already taken possession of him. We took his icy hand and covered it with kisses mingled with our tears. He made an effort to raise himself in order to bestow his blessing upon us. " Be happy, my children," he said. An hour later our excellent father was no more (May 9, 1768).

My sorrow was so overwhelming that I was unable to return to my painting for a long time. Doyen often came to see us. As he had been my father's closest friend, his visits brought us great consolation. It was owing to his persuasion that I resumed my beloved occupation, which, in fact, proved to be the only distraction capable of assuaging my sorrow and reclaiming me from my sad thoughts. It was about that time that I commenced painting from nature. I made several portraits in pastels and oils. I also drew from nature and from casts, mostly by lamp-light, with Mlle Boquet, whose acquaintance I had then made. I used to visit her in the evening at her house in the Rue St. Denis, facing the Rue de la Truanderie, where her father kept a curiosity shop. The distance was fairly long, as we were living in the Rue de Cléry opposite the Lubert mansion ; so my mother always had me accompanied.

Mlle Boquet and I would often betake ourselves, for the purpose of drawing, to the house of Briard, the painter, who lent us his models and ancient busts. Briard was an indifferent painter, although he executed several ceilings remarkable for their composition. He was, however, a very fine sketcher, a fact which induced several young people to take lessons from him. He lived at the Louvre. In order to draw as long as possible, we both used to take our lunch with us in a small basket carried by a maid. I still remember how we treated ourselves by buying from the concierge of one of the doors of the Louvre pieces of *bœuf à la mode*, which were so excellent that I cannot recall having ever eaten anything better.

Mlle Boquet was then eleven years old, while I was fourteen. We vied with each other in beauty ; for I have forgotten to tell you, dear friend, I had undergone a metamorphosis and grown pretty. Her capabilities for painting were remarkable, while my own progress was so rapid that I began to be talked about among people with the result that I had the satisfaction of making the acquaintance of Joseph Vernet. That celebrated artist gave me great encouragement and excellent advice. " My child," he said, " don't follow any system of school. Only consult the works of the great Italian and Flemish masters. But above all, work as much as you can from nature. Nature is the first of all masters. If you study it carefully, you will avoid falling into mannerisms."

I have always followed his advice, for I have never had an actual master. As for Joseph Vernet, he proved the excellence of his method by his works, which have always been and will be rightly admired.

About that time I also made the acquaintance of the Abbé Arnault, of the French Academy. He possessed a rich imagination and was passionately fond of good literature and the Arts, and it was to his conversation that I owe my enrichment in ideas, if I may use such an expression. He spoke of painting and music with the liveliest enthusiasm. He was an ardent supporter of Gluck, and later on brought that musician to my house ; for I also loved music passionately.

My mother grew proud of my looks and figure, as I had begun to put on flesh and show the freshness of youth. She would take me to the Tuileries on Sundays. She was herself still very beautiful, and since so many years have passed since then, I can tell you now that we were followed about in such a way that I was much more embarrassed thereby than flattered.

Perceiving that I was still under the impression of my cruel loss, my mother took it into her head to lead me round the picture-galleries. She showed me the Luxembourg Palace, where the gallery then contained some masterpieces by Rubens, while many rooms were full of the greatest masters.[1] These pictures have since been

[1] At present the pictures of modern French painters are displayed there I am the only one to have nothing in this collection (1835).

STUDY OF A HEAD.
Drawn by Madame Le Brun (Musée du Louvre).

To face p 23.

removed to the Museum, while those of Rubens lose much by being no longer seen in the place where they were made ; well or badly lighted pictures are like well or badly performed plays.

We used also to pay visits to private collections. Randon de Boisset possessed a gallery of Flemish and French pictures. The Duke of Praslin and the Marquis de Lévis had rich collections of the great masters of every school. M. Harent de Presle had a great number of Italian masters ; but none of these collections could be compared with that of the Palais Royal, which was brought together by the Regent and contained so many masterpieces of Italy. It was sold at the time of the Revolution, the greater part being purchased by Lord Stafford.

As soon as I set foot inside one of these rich galleries I could be truly compared to a bee, so many were the bits of knowledge and useful remembrances that I gathered for my art while intoxicating myself with delight in the contemplation of the great masters. Moreover, in order to strengthen my grasp, I copied several Rubens, some heads by Rembrandt and Van Dyck, together with girls' heads by Greuze, because the latter were extremely helpful in explaining the half-tones to be found in delicate flesh colours. Van Dyck also shows them, but more finely.

To this work I owe the important study of the gradation of light on the outstanding parts of the head. I have always admired this gradation in the heads of Raphael, which assemble, it is

23

true, all the perfections. It is only in Rome, under the beautiful sky of Italy, that one can really judge Raphael. When I was able later on to see those of his masterpieces which have never left their native land, I found Raphael superior to his immense renown.

My father left no fortune ; but I was already earning a good deal of money, having lots of portraits to paint. This, however, was insufficient to pay the expenses of our household, especially as I had to pay my brother's college fees, provide him with clothes, books, etc. So my mother found herself obliged to marry again. She married a rich jeweller, whom we had never suspected of avarice, yet who turned out immediately after the marriage to be so mean that he denied us even the necessary, although I was good-natured enough to give him all that I earned. Joseph Vernet was very much upset about it. He constantly urged me to pay a fixed sum for my board and lodging and to keep the remainder. I did nothing of the sort, however, fearing lest my mother would have to suffer from such a skin-flint.

I detested that man, the more so because he had taken possession of my father's wardrobe and wore his clothes without even troubling to have them adjusted to his own requirements. You can well imagine, my dear friend, what a sad impression he made on me.

As I have already mentioned, I had many portraits to paint, and my budding reputation already brought me the visits of a number of strangers. Several important Russians came to see me, among others the famous Count Orloff, one of the assassins of Peter III. He was a colossal man, and I remember he wore an enormous diamond on his finger.

I painted almost at once the portrait of Count Shouvaloff. He was then about sixty years old, I believe, and had been the lover of Elisabeth II. He united a benevolent politeness with a perfect manner, and as he was an excellent man, he was much sought after by the best people.

About the same time I received a visit from Mme Geoffrin, the woman who is celebrated for her salon. She used to gather together at her house all the most distinguished men of letters and artists, outstanding foreigners, and the highest gentlemen of the Court. Without birth, talents, or even much of a fortune, she had carved out for herself an unequalled position in Paris that no woman could arrive at nowadays. Having heard of me, she came to see me one morning and told me most flattering things about my person and talent. Although she was not very old at the time, I should have thought she was a hundred. Not only was she slightly bent, but her costume made her look much older. She wore an iron-grey dress and a big butterfly bonnet, decked with a black kerchief fastened under the chin. Nowadays, women of a similar age know how to make themselves look younger by the care they bestow on their toilette.

Immediately after my mother's marriage, we went to live at my stepfather's house in the Rue St. Honoré, opposite the terrace of the Palais Royal, on to which my windows opened. I often saw the Duchess de Chartres walking about the garden with her ladies, and I soon noticed that she looked at me in a kind and interested manner. I had just finished my mother's portrait, which was causing a great stir. The Duchess sent for me to paint her at her apartments. She inspired all about her with the extreme benevolence she showed towards my youthful talent, so that it was not long before I was visited by the great and beautiful Countess de Brionne and her daughter, the Princess de Lorraine, who was extremely beautiful, and then by all the great ladies of the Court and the Faubourg Saint Germain.

Since I have gone so far, dear friend, as to own that I was always stared after at the promenades and shows, even to the extent of being mobbed, you can readily understand that several admirers of my looks made me paint theirs in the hope of securing my pleasure. I was, however, so much taken up with my art that I could by no means be distracted from it. Moreover, the moral and religious principles which my mother had taught me were a shield against the seductions around me. I was lucky not to have read a single romance so far. The first I read (*Clarissa Howe*, which interested me enormously) was after my marriage. Till then I read nothing but books of piety, the moral teaching of the Holy Fathers

MOTHER-LOVE

A portrait of Madame Le Brun and her daughter.

To face p 26.

among others, of which I never grew tired, as everything is in them, and a few class-books of my brother.

With regard to the gentlemen, as soon as I realized they wished to make eyes at me, I painted them with their gaze averted ; which prevents the sitter from looking at the painter. At the least movement of their pupils in my direction, I would say : " I'm doing the eyes." That would annoy them a little, as you can imagine, but my mother, who was always with me and in my confidence, would laugh to herself.[1]

After hearing High Mass on Sundays and festivals, my mother and stepfather would take me to the Palais Royal for a walk. At that time the park was infinitely larger and more beautiful than it is at present, stifled and shrunk by the houses surrounding it on all sides. On the left-hand side there was a very broad and long avenue of enormous trees, which formed an overhead vault impenetrable to the sun's rays. It was there that fashion assembled in very grand attire. The lesser lights took refuge at a distance under the chess-board trees.

The Opéra was close by in those days, bordering on the Palace. In summer, the show ended at half-past eight o'clock, and all the elegant people came out, even before the end, to walk about

---

[1] The Marquis de Choiseul was one of them, and this fact roused my indignation, for he had just married the prettiest person in the world. She was called Mlle Raby, an American, aged sixteen. I do not believe anything more perfect has ever been seen.

the grounds. It was the fashion for women to carry very large nosegays, which, together with the scented powders on their hair, literally embalmed the air one breathed. Later, though before the Revolution, I have known these gatherings continue till two in the morning. There were musical performances by moonlight in the open. Amateurs and artists, among others Garat and Azevédo, used to sing, while others played the harp and guitar. The famous Saint-Georges played the violin. There was always a dense crowd.

It was there that I first saw the pretty and elegant Mlle Duthé, who was walking in the company of other kept women. It was not admissible in those days for a man to appear in public with those young ladies. If men joined them at the show, it was always in boxes behind grills. The English are much less delicate on that score. This same Mlle Duthé was often accompanied by an Englishman, who was so faithful that I saw them together at the show in London eighteen years afterwards. The Englishman's brother was with him, and I was told that they all three lived together. You have no idea, my dear, what the kept women of that period were like. Mlle Duthé, for instance, swallowed up millions of money. Nowadays the position of a courtesane is a lost one : no one thinks of ruining himself for a girl.

The latter word reminds me of a saying of the Duchess de Chartres, whose naïveté I like. I have already mentioned to you ·that princess, a worthy daughter of the virtuous and beneficent Duke de Penthiévre. Some time after her marriage she was standing at the window, when one of her gentlemen, seeing some of those girls go by, remarked : " There are some girls."—" How can you know they are not married ? " asked the Duchess in all her candid ignorance.

It was impossible for Mlle Boquet and me to walk down that great avenue of the Palais Royal without attracting attention. We were then between sixteen and seventeen years old. Mlle Boquet was very beautiful. At nineteen she had smallpox, the news of which affliction awoke such interest in all classes of society that crowds of people flocked to make inquiries after her condition, while a large number of carriages were constantly at her door. In those days Beauty was in truth a thing of celebrity. Mlle Boquet was remarkably gifted for painting, but she abandoned it almost entirely after she had married M. Filleul, when the Queen appointed her wardress of the Château de la Muette.

How can I mention this lovable woman to you without recalling her tragic end ? Alas ! I remember that when I was on the point of leaving France in order to escape the horror I foresaw, Mme Filleul said to me : " You are wrong to leave. I will stay, because I believe in the happiness which the Revolution will bring us."

And that Revolution led her to the scaffold ! She was still at the Château de la Muette when

found a pretext for arresting Mme Chalgrin and
Mme Filleul, who were accused of *burning the
candles of the nation*. They were both guillotined
a few days later.

Here I will end this sad letter.

Ce vifage vaut mieux que toutes vos chanfons

THE PALACE GALLERY.

To face p. 30.

CHAPTER III

I WILL GO ON, dear friend, with the story
of my outings in what I may call old Paris
on account of the great many changes which
that city has undergone since the days of my
youth. One of the most frequented promenades
was that of the Boulevards du Temple. Every
day, especially Thursday, saw hundreds of carriages coming and going or standing about the
avenues where there are now cafés and parades.
Young people on horseback pranced about them,
as at Longchamp, which was already in existence.[1]

One side of the boulevard, where the Café Turc is now situated, afforded a sight which made me burst into fits of laughter many a time. It was a long row of old women from the Marais Institution, all solemnly sitting on chairs, and whose cheeks were so daubed with rouge that they looked like dolls. As at that time only women of high rank were permitted to wear red, these ladies considered themselves obliged to exercise the privilege to its fullest extent. One of our friends who was acquainted with most of them, told us their only occupation was playing lotto from morn to night and that coming back from Versailles one day, he was asked for news by some of them. He replied that M. de La Pérouse was about to start out on a journey round the world. " Indeed ! " exclaimed the mistress of the house, " that man must be sadly in need of a job ! "

Later on, a good while after my marriage, I went to many shows on that boulevard. The one I saw and enjoyed most was that of the puppets of Carlo Perico. These marionettes were so well made and so dexterously manipulated that they sometimes achieved a perfect illusion. My daughter, who was six years old at most, and whom I took with me, had no doubt at first of their being alive. When I told her the contrary, I remember taking her a few days later to the Comédie Française, where my box was fairly remote from the stage. " And those, Mamma," she said to me, " are they alive ? "

The Colisée was still a very fashionable place of gathering. It consisted of an immense circle built in one of the great squares of the Champs Elysées. In the middle was a lake of limpid water on which boating tournaments took place. People strolled about the broad, sandy avenues which were ornamented with seats. At nightfall, everybody left the garden and entered an immense hall where an excellent programme of music was provided every evening. Mlle Lemaure, a celebrity of that time, sang there several times, as did also many other famous women singers. The broad terrace which led to this hall was the rendezvous of all the gilded youth of Paris, who stood under the lighted porch and let no woman pass without making her the subject of an epigram. One evening as I was coming down the steps with my mother, the Duke de Chartres, since known as Philippe-Egalité, stood there with his arm in that of the Marquis de Genlis, his companion in orgy, while the unfortunate women who attracted their attention did not escape the most infamous sarcasms. " Ah ! as for that one," said the Duke in a very loud voice as he pointed to me, " there's nothing to be said." This remark, which was heard by many persons besides myself, gave me so great a satisfaction that I remember it even to-day with a certain amount of pleasure.

About the same time there existed on the Boulevard du Temple a place called the Vauxhall l'Été, the garden of which was nothing more than a large space for walking about in, and

round which were covered tiers where fine people
used to sit. They forgathered in the daytime
in summer, and the evening would end up with a
very fine display of fireworks.

All these places were even more fashionable
than Tivoli is at present. It is somewhat surprising that Parisians, whose only promenades are
the Tuileries and the Luxembourg Gardens, should
have abandoned these half-urban, half-rural establishments where one could go for a breath of air
and ices in the evening.

My wretched stepfather—annoyed, no doubt, by
the public tributes to my mother's beauty and
I venture to say, to my own as well—forbade us
to go to the promenades, and told us one day
that he was going to rent a country house. My
heart beat for joy at the announcement, for I
was deeply in love with the country. I wished
all the more to stay there as I felt a great need
for it, since I was then sleeping at the foot of
my mother's bed, in an alcove where the daylight
never penetrated. Indeed, the first thing I did
in the morning in all weathers was to open the
window for a breath of fresh air.

So my stepfather rented a little house at Chaillot
and we used to go there on Saturday, returning
to Paris on Monday morning. Heavens ! what a
country house ! Just imagine, my dear, a tiny
vicarage garden ; no trees, no other shelter from
the sun except a little bower where my stepfather
had planted some beans and nasturtiums which
wouldn't grow. Moreover, we had only a quarter

34

WAVERING VIRTUE.

From the painting by Madame Le Brun.

To face p 35.

of that charming garden, for it was divided into four by small sticks, the three other parts being let to some shop-fellows, who amused themselves there every Sunday with bird-shooting. The perpetual noise of this brought me into a state of despair. Besides which, I was dreadfully afraid of being killed by the clumsy fellows, who couldn't shoot straight at all.

I could not understand how one could call so miserable a place a country house. I found it so wearisome that I yawn at the very memory of it in writing this. At last, however, my guardian angel sent me a friend of my mother's, Mme Suzanne, who came to dine at Chaillot with her husband one day. They felt sorry for me and my weariness, and sometimes took me out for wonderful excursions. Unfortunately M. Suzanne could not be relied upon to come every Sunday, as he suffered from a strange disease. Every other day he would shut himself up in his room, refusing to see anybody, even his wife, and declining to speak or eat. The next day, however, he would recover his merriment and habitual manners. So it was necessary to keep oneself well posted with the state of his health in order to make any arrangements with him.

We went first of all to Marly-le-Roi, and there I realized for the first time how enchanting a place could be. On each side of the superb château were six pavilions, connected with each other by tunnels of jasmine and honeysuckle. Magnificent cascades of water fell from a mountain at the rear of the château and formed an immense lake on which swam graceful swans. The fine trees, clumps of verdure, fountains and spirts of water, one of which rose so high that it was lost from sight, were all on a grand, majestic scale that reminded one of Louis XIV. The sight of this ravishing abode made such an impression on me that I often returned there after my marriage. One morning I met the Queen walking in the park with several ladies of her Court. They were all wearing white dresses and were so young and pretty that they looked like an apparition. I was with my mother, and started to go away, when the Queen very kindly stopped me and desired me to go on walking wherever I pleased. Alas! when I returned to France in 1802, I hastened to see my noble, laughing Marly once again. Palace, trees, cascades, fountain, everything had disappeared.

M. and Mme Suzanne took me to see the château and park at Sceaux. The section of the park adjoining the château was laid out in a regular fashion with lawns and flower-beds like the garden of the Tuileries. The other section had no symmetrical design, but a great stretch of water and the finest trees I have ever seen made it much more preferable, in my opinion. The goodness of the owner of that magnificent abode was shown by the fact that the park was open to the public. The Duke de Penthièvre had always desired that the public should be admitted. On Sundays especially, the park was much frequented

It was very distressing for me to leave those magnificent gardens in order to return to our sad Chaillot. However, with the arrival of winter we went to Paris, where I made pleasant use of the time which my work left me. Since the age of fifteen I had been going about in high society. I was acquainted with our foremost artists and received invitations on all sides. I well remember dining for the first time in town with the sculptor Le Moine, who was then much in vogue. He was extremely simple, but he showed good taste in gathering under his roof a great number of famous and distinguished men. His two daughters carried out the rôle of hostesses to perfection. It was there that I saw the celebrated Lekain, who frightened me with his lowering, wild aspect, his enormous eyebrows augmenting the graceless expression of his face. He never spoke, but ate enormously. Next to him and opposite me sat the prettiest woman in Paris, Mme de Bonneuil (mother of Mme Regnault Saint-Jean d'Angely), who was as fresh as a rose. Her gentle beauty was so charming that I was unable to take my eyes off her, especially as she had been placed near my husband, who was as ugly as a monkey, while the faces of Lekain and M. de Bonneuil formed a sort of double foil, which she certainly did not require.

It was at Le Moine's house that I made the acquaintance of Gerbier, the celebrated advocate. Mme de Roissy, his daughter, was very beautiful and one of the first women I painted. Grétry and Letour, the famous pastel painter, were often present at these dinners, which were very merry. It was the custom of the time to sing at dessert. Mme de Bonneuil, who had a charming voice, sang duets by Grétry with her husband, after which came the turn of the young ladies, who, it must be admitted, felt like martyrs. They were seen to grow pale, tremble and often sing out of tune. In spite of these little discords, the dinner would end in merriment and one went away with regret, being loath to call for one's carriage on rising from table as is done nowadays.

I cannot, however, speak of the dinners of to-day except from hearsay, as a short while after the one I have mentioned I gave up dining out. The daylight hours were really too valuable for me to sacrifice them to society, while a little event occurred which made me decide of a sudden never to go out at night again. I had accepted an invitation to dine with the Princess de Rohan-Rochefort. When I was dressed and ready to enter my carriage, the idea occurred to me to take another look at a portrait I had commenced that morning. I was wearing a white satin dress, which I had put on for the first time. I sat down on a chair in front of my easel entirely unaware that my palette was on it. My dress was in such a state when I got up that I was obliged to stay at home, and from that time I resolved nevermore to accept invitations except to supper.

The suppers of the Princess de Rohan-Rochefort were charming. Her society was chiefly made up of the beautiful Countess de Brionne, her

LA PROMENADE DU SOIR

Jeunes Beautés qui fuyez l'esclavage,   Mais d'un Bouquet n'acceptez point l'hommage,
Vous pouvez écouter des propos séducteurs: Souvent l'Amour s'est caché dans les fleurs.

THE EVENING PROMENADE.

To face p. 39.

daughter, the Princess de Lorraine, the Duke de Choiseul, Cardinal de Rohan, M. de Rulhières, author of *Les Disputes*. But the most likeable of all the guests was undoubtedly the Duke de Lauzun, whose wit and merriment were beyond compare and charmed everybody. The evening was often spent with music and sometimes I sang, accompanying myself with a guitar. Supper was at half-past ten, and never more than ten or twelve sat down at table. The guests vied with one another in wit and pleasantness. I could only listen, as you may readily understand, and although I was too young to appreciate the charm of the conversation, I found it put me off many others.

I have often told you, my dear friend, that my life as a girl was like no other. Not only was I received and sought after in the salons on account of my talent, weak though I found it in comparison with the great masters, but I sometimes received proofs of public good will, so to speak, which gave me much joy, I frankly admit. For instance, having made the portraits of Cardinal de Fleury and La Bruyére from some engravings of the time, I offered them to the French Academy, who sent me back the following letter through d'Alembert, the chief secretary :

Mademoiselle,
    The French Academy has received with all possible acknowledgment the letter which you have addressed to it, together with the beautiful portraits of Fleury and La Bruyère which you have kindly sent it in order that they may be hung in its assembly hall, where it has long desired to see them. In reproducing for it the features of two men whose name it holds

in high esteem, these two portraits will constantly remind it, Mademoiselle, of all that it owes and is flattered to owe to you. Moreover, they will provide it with a lasting monument of your rare talents with which it was acquainted through the voice of the public and which are enhanced in you by wit, graciousness, and the most agreeable modesty.

Wishing to reply to so praiseworthy an action as yours in the most fitting manner, the company begs you, Mademoiselle, to accept the right of entry to all its public assemblies. This was unanimously resolved upon at its assembly yesterday, and was immediately inserted in its registers, while I was charged to convey the assembly's decision to you and to offer you its thanks. This commission is all the more agreeable to me because it affords me the opportunity to assure you, Mademoiselle, of my high esteem for your talents and person, an esteem which I share with all persons of good taste and sound reason.

I have the honour respectfully to be, Mademoiselle, your very humble and very obedient servant,

D'ALEMBERT,
Permanent Secretary to the French Academy.

PARIS, *August* 10, 1775.

The offer of these two portraits to the Academy soon brought me the honour of a visit from d'Alembert, a small, cold, and dry man though meticulously polite. He stayed a long time and inspected my atelier, saying all sorts of flattering things to me. I have never forgotten how, just after his departure, a grand lady who had been present, asked me whether I had painted from nature the portraits of La Bruyére and Fleury that had just been talked about. "I'm a little too young for that," I replied, unable to suppress a laugh, but very glad for the poor lady's sake that the Academician was no longer present.

CHAPTER IV

MY STEPFATHER having retired from business, we went to reside at a mansion called Lubert, in the Rue de Cléry. M. Le Brun had just bought this house and was living there. As soon as we were settled, I went to see the magnificent pictures of every school of painting with which his apartment was filled. I was delighted to have a neighbour who afforded me every chance of consulting the works of the great masters. M. Le Brun was extremely kind in lending me pictures of admirable beauty and rare value for the purpose of making copies. It was to him, therefore, that I owed the strongest lessons I was able to get, till at the end of six months he begged for my hand in marriage. I was far from any wish to marry, although he was very well made and good-looking. I was then twenty years old and leading a life free from any anxiety as to my future, for I was earning a good deal of money and felt no desire whatever to get married. But my mother, who thought

M. Le Brun to be very rich, unceasingly urged
me not to refuse such a profitable match, and at
last I consented to the marriage,[1] desiring above
all to escape from the torment of living with my
stepfather, whose bad humour had grown more
and more each day since his idleness. So small,
however, was my enthusiasm to give up my freedom,
that on the way to the church I kept saying to
myself : " Shall I say yes ? Shall I say no ? " Alas,
I said " yes," and changed my old troubles for new
ones.

Not that M. Le Brun was a bad man : his
character showed a mixture of gentleness and
vivacity ; he was very obliging towards everybody—
in a word, likeable enough ; but his unbridled
passion for women of bad morals, joined to his
fondness for gambling, brought about the ruin
of his fortune as well as mine, which was entirely
in his keeping. Indeed, when I left France in
1789, I had not so much as twenty francs of income
though I had earned more than a million. He
had squandered the lot.

For some time my marriage was kept secret
M. Le Brun had intended marrying the daughter
of a Dutchman with whom he did much business
in paintings, and begged me not to announce
our marriage until he concluded his affairs.
agreed to this with all the more willingness because
I regretted giving up my maiden name, by which
I was very well known. Though the mystery
lasted but a short while, it was destined to have

---

[1] January 11, 1776, at the church of St. Eustache, Paris.

VIEW OF PASSY, FROM THE ÎLE DES CYGNES.

From a drawing by Le Veau.

To face p. 42.

an evil effect on my future. Many persons, under the impression that I was merely about to marry M. Le Brun, visited me with the purpose of dissuading me from such a foolish act. One of them was Aubert, the Crown jeweller, who said to me in a friendly manner : " You would do better to tie a stone round your neck and throw yourself into the river than to marry Le Brun." Another was the Duchess d'Aremberg, accompanied by Mme de Canillac and Mme de Souza, wife of the Portuguese Ambassador, all three so young and pretty, who brought me their tardy advice a fortnight after my marriage. " In the name of Heaven," said the Duchess, " don't marry M. Le Brun. You would be too unhappy ! " Then she related to me a lot of things which I was lucky enough not to believe altogether, although they have since turned out to be only too true ; but my mother, who was present, could scarcely hold back her tears.

Finally the announcement of my marriage put an end to these sad warnings, from which my habitual gaiety had suffered little, thanks to my dear painting. I was unable to cope with all the demands for portraits which poured in from all quarters, and although M. Le Brun had already acquired the habit of pocketing the fees, he even took it into his head to make me take some pupils in order to increase our income. I yielded to his wish without troubling to think it over, and I soon had several young ladies to whom I showed how to paint eyes, noses and faces, which

43

constantly needed touching up, much to my disgust and the neglect of my own work.

One of my pupils was Mlle Emilie De La Ville Le Roulx, who afterwards married M. Benoist, Director of Law, and for whom Demoustiers wrote *Lettres sur la Mythologie.* She made pastel paintings of heads, in which one could already discern the talent which has given her a just celebrity. Mlle Emilie was the youngest of my pupils, most of whom were older than myself, a fact which detracted enormously from the respect which the head of a school should impose. I had set up the atelier of these young ladies in a disused hayloft, the ceiling of which displayed very thick beams. One morning I discovered my pupils had tied a rope to one of the beams and were swinging to their hearts' content. I put on a serious look and reproved them, making a superb speech on wasting time ; whereupon I felt a strong desire to try the swing myself and was soon amusing myself on it more than all the others. You can imagine that such manners made it very difficult for me to overawe my pupils, and this inconvenience, together with the tedium of returning to the A B C of my art in correcting their studies, soon obliged me to give the school up.

The obligation to leave my dear atelier for a few hours increased, I believe, my fondness for work. I did not lay down my brushes till night was quite fallen, and the number of portraits I painted at that period is really amazing. As I greatly disliked the style of dress worn by the

44

women at that time, I did my best to make it a little more picturesque, and whenever I obtained the confidence of my models I delighted in draping them after my fancy.

People had not yet taken to wearing shawls, but I made use of large scarves, lightly interlaced round the body and over the arms, whereby I tried to imitate the beautiful style of the draperies of Raphael and Dominichino, as you may have noticed in several of my portraits in Russia, especially in that of my *Girl Playing the Guitar.* Moreover, I loathed the use of powder. I persuaded the beautiful Duchess de Gramont-Caderousse not to use any when sitting for her portrait.[1] Her hair was as black as ebony, and I divided it up into irregular curls on the forehead. After my sitting, which ended at the hour of dinner, the Duchess retained her coiffure and went in it to the theatre. Such a pretty woman was sure to set the tone, and indeed the fashion grew gently, till at last it became general. This reminds me that when I painted the Queen in 1786 I begged her not to put on any powder and to part her hair on the forehead. "I shall be the last to follow such a fashion," the Queen said with laughter; "I don't wish it to be said that I have invented it in order to hide my large forehead."

I tried as well as I could to give the women I painted the attitude and expression of their physiognomy. As for those who had none, I

[1] Exhibited at the Salon of 1785.

painted them like dreamers reclining heedlessly
However, one must suppose they were satisfied
for I was unable to cope with the demands. I
was difficult to get a place in my waiting list
In a word, I was the fashion. Everything seemed
to have conspired to make me so. You may wel
judge of the fact from the following scene, which
I always recall with flattery. Some time afte:
my marriage, I was present at a sitting of the
French Academy, when La Harpe read his speech
on the talents of women. When he came to the
following highly exaggerated lines, which I ther
heard for the first time—

> Le Brun, de la beauté le peintre et le modèle,
> Moderne Rosalba, mais plus brillante qu'elle,
> Joint la voix de Favart au souris de Venus, etc. [1]—

the author of *Warwick* turned his gaze towards me
Whereupon the entire public, not excepting th
Duchess de Chartres and the King of Swede
who were present, stood up and faced me, applaud
ing me so frantically that I was almost overcom
with confusion.

These pleasures of conceit, which I relate t
you, dear friend, because you demanded I shoul
tell you everything, cannot be compared to th
enjoyment I felt on learning, two years after m
marriage, that I was with child. But here yo
will see how much I failed in foresight owing t
my extreme affection for my art, for in spite o

[1] "Le Brun, the painter and model of beauty,
The Rosalba of our days, but more brilliant than she,
Unites the voice of Favart with the smile of Venus," etc.

HEAD-DRESSES OF THE XVIIIᴛʜ CENTURY.

To face p. 46.

my happiness at the idea of becoming a mother, I let the nine months of my labour go by without giving the least thought to the preparation of the things necessary to child-birth. On the day my daughter was born I did not quit my atelier, and continued working at my *Venus Tying the Wings of Love*, in the intervals between the throes.

Mme de Verdun, my oldest friend, came to see me in the morning. She realized that I would be brought to bed during the day, and as she knew me, she asked me whether I was provided with all that was necessary ; to which I replied, with a look of astonishment, that I didn't know at all what was necessary. " That's just like you," she said, " you are a real boy. I warn you that you will be brought to bed this evening."—" No, no ! " I exclaimed, " I have a sitting to-morrow. I will not go to bed to-day." Without troubling to reply, Mme de Verdun left me for a moment to send out for the man midwife, who arrived almost at once. I sent him away, but he hid in the house till the evening, when at ten o'clock my daughter came into the world. I will not attempt to describe the joy which overwhelmed me when I heard my baby cry. Every mother knows that joy ; it is all the more lively because it is accompanied by the repose following the atrocious birth pangs. I think M. Dubois expressed the thought perfectly when he said : " Happiness is finding interest in calm."

During my pregnancy I had painted the Duchess de Mazarin, who was no longer young,

but still beautiful. My daughter had the same
kind of eyes and resembled her amazingly. This
Duchess de Mazarin was said to have been endowed
at her birth by three fairies : Riches, Beauty, and
Ill-Luck. It is perfectly true that the poor woman
could never undertake anything, not even giving
a party, without some misfortune or other turning
up. Many misfortunes of her life have been
related, but here is one less known : One evening
while entertaining sixty persons to supper, she
contrived to have on the table an enormous pie
in which a hundred small birds were shut up alive
At a sign from the Duchess the pie was opened and
all the frantic little creatures flew out, dashing into
faces and clinging to the hair of the women, who
were all carefully attired and hair-dressed. You can
imagine the tempers, the shouts ! The unfortunate
birds could not be got rid of, and were such a
nuisance that the guests were obliged to leave the
table, cursing such a foolish flight of fancy.

The Duchess de Mazarin had grown so very
stout that it took ages to do up her corsets. A
visitor coming to see her one day while she was
being laced, one of her women ran to the door
and cried out : "Don't come in till we've arranged
the rolls of flesh." I remember that this excessive
plumpness aroused the admiration of the Turkish
Ambassadors. When they were asked at the Opéra
which woman they liked best among those who
filled the boxes, they replied without hesitation
that the Duchess de Mazarin was the most
beautiful because she was the fattest.

48

Talking of ambassadors, I must not forget to tell you how I painted two diplomats, who in spite of being copper-coloured had splendid heads. In 1788 ambassadors were sent to Paris by the Emperor Tippoo-Sahib. I saw these Indians at the Opéra, and they appeared to me so unusually picturesque that I wished to paint their portraits. Having informed them of my desire, I learnt that they would never consent to be painted except at the request of the King, so I obtained this favour from His Majesty. I went with canvas and colours to the house they were living at, for they wished to be painted at home. On my arrival one of them brought some rose-water and sprinkled it on my hands. Then the greater of them, who was called Davich Khan, gave me a sitting. I painted him standing with his hand in his dagger. He posed so agreeably that I was able to do everything as it was—drapery, hands, etc. I put the picture in another room to dry and began the portrait of the old ambassador sitting with his son beside him. The father especially had a splendid head. Both were dressed in white muslin robes, sprinkled with gold flowers. I finished this picture at the time with the exception of the background and the bottom of the robes.

Mme de Bonneuil, to whom I had spoken of my sittings, wanted very much to meet these ambassadors. They invited us both to dinner, and we accepted the invitation out of sheer curiosity. Entering the dining-room, we were

somewhat surprised to find the dinner served c
the floor, and we were thus obliged to do as the
did, lying almost flat round the low table. The
offered us with their hands what they took fro
the dishes, one of which contained a fricassee
sheep's feet with white sauce, very spicy, while tl
other held a sort of ragout. As you can imagin
it was a sad meal. We loathed watching them u
their bronzed hands in the place of spoons.

These ambassadors had brought with them
young man who spoke French slightly. Durir
the sittings Mme de Bonneuil taught him
sing *Annette à l'age de quinze ans.* When v
went to take leave, this young man recited I
song and expressed his sorrow at leaving us, sa
ing: "Ah! how my heart weeps!" Which
thought very Oriental and very well said.

When the portrait of Davich Khan was dry,
sent for it. He had hidden it, however, behi
his bed and refused to part with it, declarii
that a soul was due to inhabit it, according to t
Mahometan belief. This refusal gave rise
some pretty verses addressed to me, which I co
here:

A Madame Le Brun.

Au sujet du portrait de Davich Khan et du préjugé des Orient
contre la peinture.

Ce n'est point aux climats où regnent les sultans
Que le marbre s'anime et la toile respire.
   Les préjugés de leurs imans
   Du dieu des arts ont renversé l'empire.

VIEW OF THE PALAIS-BOURBON AND THE COURS LA REINE FROM THE
TUILERIES TERRACE.

From a drawing by Lespinasse in 1778.

To face p. 51.

Ils ont rêvé qu'Allah, jaloux de nos talents,
Doit en jugeant les mondes et les âges
Donner une âme á ces images.
Qui sauvent la beauté des ravages du temps.
Sublime Allah ! tu ris de cette erreur impie !
Tu conviendras, voyant cette copie,
Où l'art de la nature a surpris les secrets,
Que comme toi, le génie a ses flammes ;
Et que Le Brun, en peignant des portraits,
Sait aussi leur donner une âme.[1]

I was unable to get hold of my picture except by trickery. When the Ambassador discovered it was gone, he blamed his valet and wanted to kill him. The interpreter was at his wits' end to make him understand that it was not usual to kill one's valet in Paris, and he was obliged to tell him that the King of France had asked for the portrait.

Both these pictures were hung at the Salon of 1789. After the death of M. Le Brun, who claimed all my works, they were sold and I do not know who owns them to-day.

[1] To Madame Le Brun.

A propos of the portrait of Davich Khan and the prejudice of Orientals against painting.

" It is not in climates where the sultans reign that marble comes to life and canvas breathes. The prejudices of their priests have overthrown the empire of the god of Art. They have imagined that at the day of judgment Allah, being jealous of our talents, must give a soul to likenesses, which save beauty from the ravages of time. Sublime Allah ! Thou laughest at this impious error ! Thou wilt agree, on seeing this copy, wherein Art has discovered the secrets of Nature, that, like Thee, genius has its lustre ; and that Le Brun, painting portraits, knows how to give them a soul."

CHAPTER V

IT WAS IN THE YEAR 1779, my dear
friend, that I painted my first portrait of
the Queen, who was then in all the glory of
her youth and beauty. Marie-Antoinette was tall,
admirably shaped, and fairly plump. Her arms
were superb, her hands small and of perfect shape,
while her feet were charming. She walked better
than any other woman in France, holding her
head well up with a majesty that stamped her as
sovereign in the midst of all her Court, without,
however, detracting in any way from what was
kind and gentle in her aspect. It is difficult,
however, to convey to anyone who never saw
the Queen an adequate idea of her noble traits
and many graceful qualities. Her features were
not at all regular ; she took after her family with
the long narrow face peculiar to the Austrian
nation. Her eyes were not large, and their colour
was almost blue. Her expression was bright and
gentle, her nose fine and pretty, her mouth not
too big, though the lips were rather strong. The

52

most remarkable thing about her face was the splendour of her complexion.

I have never seen another so brilliant; for " brilliant " is the word : her skin was so transparent that it had no shading. I was unable to reproduce its effect to my satisfaction ; I lacked the colours necessary to paint the freshness and fine tones, which I have never found in any other woman.

At my first sitting, the Queen's imposing aspect overawed me tremendously ; but Her Majesty spoke to me so kindly that this impression was soon dissipated. It was then that I painted the portrait representing her with a large basket, dressed in a satin robe and holding a rose in her hand. This portrait was intended for her brother, the Emperor Joseph II. The Queen ordered two copies of it, one for the Empress of Russia, the other for her apartments at Versailles or Fontainebleau.

I painted several other portraits of the Queen at various times. In one of them I merely painted her as far as the knees, dressed in an orange-coloured robe and standing before a table, on which she was in the act of arranging some flowers in a vase. It is easy to realize that I preferred to paint her without grand attire and, above all, without a large basket. These portraits were given to her friends, some of them to ambassadors. One of them shows her wearing a straw hat and dressed in a white muslin robe, the sleeves of which were crimpled crosswise but fairly tight. When this portrait was exhibited at the Salon, the evil-minded did not fail to say that the Queen had had herself painted *en chemise* ; for it was the year 1786, and slander had already begun to make her its butt.

Nevertheless, this portrait had a great success. Towards the end of the exhibition a little play, called, I believe, *La Réunion des Arts*, was performed at the Vaudeville. Brongniart the architect and his wife, who were in the author's confidence, engaged a box and came to fetch me for the first performance. As I was entirely unaware of the surprise which had been prepared for me, you can judge of my emotion when the turn came to Painting and I saw the actress copy me in a surprising manner in the act of painting the Queen's portrait. At the same moment everybody in the boxes and parterre turned towards me and applauded me tumultuously. And I do not believe it is possible for anyone to be so moved and grateful as I was that evening.

The bashfulness I had felt at my first encounter with the Queen completely yielded to the gracious kindness which she always showed me. When Her Majesty heard that I possessed a nice voice, she gave me few sittings without making me accompany her in several of Grétry's duets ; for she loved music immensely, though her voice was not quite accurate. As for her conversation, it would be hard for me to describe all its grace and kindness. I do not believe Queen Marie-Antoinette ever failed to say something pleasant to those who had the honour of approaching her,

54

THE BOX AT THE OPÉRA.
After Moreau, junior.

To face p 55.

while the kindness she always showed to me is one of my sweetest memories.

One day I happened to miss the appointment for a sitting which she had fixed. I was then well advanced in my second pregnancy and had suddenly felt ill. The following day I hastened to Versailles to offer my excuses. The Queen was not expecting me and had ordered her coach for a drive. The coach was the first thing I noticed on entering the courtyard of the palace. Nevertheless, I went up to speak to gentlemen of the chamber. One of them, M. Campan,[1] received me in a cold, blunt manner, saying in a loud, angry voice: "It was yesterday, Madam, that Her Majesty expected you, and it is quite certain she is going for her drive and quite certain she will not give you a sitting." When I replied that I merely came to receive Her Majesty's orders for another day, he went to the Queen, who made me enter her cabinet at once. Her Majesty was just finishing her toilet. She held a book in her hand while going over a lesson with her daughter. My heart beat fast, for I was as much afraid as I was wrong. The Queen turned towards me and said very sweetly: "I waited for you all the morning yesterday. What happened to you?"—"Alas! Madam," I replied, "I was so unwell that it was impossible for me to obey Your Majesty's orders. I have come to-day

---

[1] This M. Campan was always talking about the Queen. Once, when he was dining at my house, my daughter, who was then seven years old, said to me very softly: "Mamma, is that gentleman the King?"

in order to receive them, and will go away at once."—" No ! no ! Don't go away ! " replied the Queen. " I will not allow you to make this journey for nothing." She dismissed her carriage and gave me a sitting.

I remember that in my anxiety to respond to this kindness I took hold of my box of paints with such eagerness that it was upset. My brushes and pencils were scattered on the floor. I stooped to pick them up. " Leave them, leave them ! " said the Queen. " You are too far gone with child to stoop." And in spite of all I could say, she picked them all up herself.

When the Court paid its last visit to Fontaine-bleau in grand style, as custom demanded, I went to enjoy the sight. I saw the Queen in grand attire, covered with diamonds. In the brilliant sunshine she seemed to me really dazzling. As she walked along, her head, uplifted on its beautiful Greek neck, made her look so imposing and majestic that one was reminded of a goddess in the midst of her nymphs.

At the first sitting Her Majesty gave me on her return from that journey, I ventured to mention the impression I had received and to tell the Queen how much the nobility of her aspect was enhanced by the high bearing of her head. She replied in a joking manner : " If I were not Queen, they would say I looked haughty ; is i not so ? "

The Queen spared no pains to train her children in the graceful and pleasant manners which endeared her so much to all who surrounded her. I have seen her when making her daughter the Princess, then six years old, dine with a little peasant girl whom she was taking care of, desire that the latter should be served first, saying to her daughter : "You must do her the honours."

The last sitting I had with Her Majesty was at the Trianon, where I painted her head for the large picture with her children. I remember that Baron de Breteuil, then a minister, was present and during the entire sitting never stopped backbiting all the women of the Court. He must have believed me to be either deaf or very good-natured, not to fear I might report some of his evil remarks to the persons concerned. The fact is, it has never occurred to me to repeat a single one of them, though I have forgotten none.

Having painted the head of the Queen, besides the separate studies of the first Dauphin, the Princess Royal and the Duke of Normandy, I immediately set to work on my picture and finished it for the Salon of 1788. The sight of the frame being carried in alone gave rise to scores of unpleasant remarks. "Voilà le déficit," they said, besides many other things which were repeated to me and forewarned me of the bitterest criticisms.

At last I sent my picture. I had not the courage, however, to go with it in order to know its fate at once, so great was my fear of its being ill received by the public. My fear, in fact, gave me a fever. I locked myself in my room, and was there praying to Heaven for the success of *my* Royal Family, when my brother and a host of friends came to tell me that I was gaining universal approbation.

After the Salon the King ordered the picture to be taken to Versailles, where M. d'Angiviller, the then Minister for Arts and director of the royal buildings, presented me to His Majesty. Louis XVI very kindly talked with me a long while and told me that he was very pleased, adding, as he looked again at my work: " I have no great knowledge of painting, but you make me fond of it."

My picture was hung in one of the rooms of the Palace at Versailles, and the Queen always passed it on her way to and from Mass. After the death of the Dauphin, at the beginning of 1789, the sight of it reminded her so vividly of her cruel loss that she was unable to cross the room without shedding tears. She then told M. d'Angiviller to have the picture removed, but with her habitual grace she took care to let me know at once the reason for its removal. It is to the Queen's sensibility that I owe the preservation of my picture, for the low jades and bandits who came a short while after to fetch their Majesties, would certainly have lacerated it, as they did the Queen's bed, which was cut right through.

I never had the pleasure of seeing Marie-Antoinette after the last ball at Versailles. This ball was given in the Court theatre. The box in which I found myself placed was near enough

VIEW OF THE CHAILLOT FIRE-STATION FROM THE GROS-CAILLOU.

From a drawing by Lallemand.

To face p. 58.

to the Queen to allow of my hearing what she said. She was very agitated, and invited the young gentlemen of the Court, such as M. de Lameth and others, to dance, all of whom refused, so that most of the set-dances could not be arranged. The conduct of these gentlemen struck me as being most unbecoming. Their refusal somehow seemed to me like a sort of revolt, pointing to something yet more serious. The Revolution was on its way ; it broke out the following year.

With the exception of the Count d'Artois, I painted successively the whole Royal Family, the French royal children, the King's brother (later, Louis XVIII), his wife, the Countess d'Artois, and the Princess Elisabeth. The features of the latter were not regular, but her face had the kindliest expression, while her great freshness was remarkable. Altogether she had the charm of a pretty shepherdess. Of course you know, dear friend, that the Princess Elisabeth was an angel of goodness. How often was I privileged to witness her good deeds towards the unfortunate ! Her heart sheltered all the virtues. Indulgent, modest, sensible and devoted, she showed in the Revolution an heroic courage. This gentle Princess was seen to walk in front of the cannibals who came to murder the Queen, saying : " They will take me for her ! "

In painting the portrait of the King's brother I was able to make the acquaintance of a Prince whose fine mind and instruction could be praised without flattery. It was impossible not to find pleasure in the conversation of Louis XVIII, who discoursed on all subjects with as much good taste as knowledge. Sometimes, by way of variety, no doubt, he would sing to me during the sittings songs which, without being unseemly, were so common that I could not understand by what channel such silly things arrived at the Court. His voice was as false as any on earth. " How do you think I sing, Madame Le Brun ? " he said to me one day.—" Like a Prince, sir," I replied.

The Marquis de Montesquiou, his equerry, sent a very fine carriage with eight horses to take me to Versailles and to bring me back with my mother, whom I had asked to accompany me. All along the way people stood at their windows to see me pass. Everybody raised his hat. I was amused by the homage paid to the eight horses and to the rider who went in front, for when I arrived in Paris, I took a cab and no one paid any further attention to me.

The King's brother was then what is called a Liberal (in the moderate sense of the word, of course). He and his followers formed a party at the Court quite distinct from that of the King. So I was by no means surprised during the Revolution to see the Marquis de Montesquiou appointed General-in-Chief of the Republican Army of Savoy. I had only to recall the strange things I heard him say in my presence, not to speak of the remarks he so openly indulged in against the Queen and all she loved. As for the King's

60

brother himself, the newspapers tell us how he went to the National Assembly and declared that he did not come to take his seat as a *prince*, but as a *citizen*. For all that, I do not believe that such a declaration would have been sufficient to save his head, and that he did the right thing a little later in leaving France.

About the same time I painted the portrait of the Princess de Lamballe. Though not pretty, she appeared to be so at a distance. She had small features, a dazzling fresh complexion, glorious fair hair and plenty of elegance about all her person. The dreadful end of that unfortunate Princess is well known, as also the devotion to which she was sacrificed ; for, being out of all peril at Turin in 1793, she returned to France as soon as she learnt that the Queen was in danger.

You see I have gone far beyond the year 1779, my dear friend. But I preferred to tell you in a single letter of my relations as an artist with all these great personages, of whom none survives to-day except the Count d'Artois (Charles X) and the unfortunate daughter of Marie-Antoinette.

IN 1782 M. LE BRUN took me to Flanders, where business called him. The superb collection of pictures belonging to Prince Charles was then being sold, and we went to see the exhibition. I found there several ladies of the Court, who received me with great kindness, one of them being the Duchess d'Aremberg, whom I had seen a good deal in Paris. I was most delighted, however, to meet Prince de Ligne, with whom I was as yet unacquainted, and who has left a sort of historical reputation for wit and affability. He invited us to inspect his gallery, where I admired several masterpieces, mostly portraits by Van Dyck and heads by Rubens, as he owned but few Italian pictures. He desired also to receive us at his superb mansion Bel-Oeil. I remember he took us up into a belvedere, built at the top of a height dominating his lands and the surrounding country. The perfect air and

62

D'ALEMBERT.

From a drawing by Cochin.

To face p. 62.

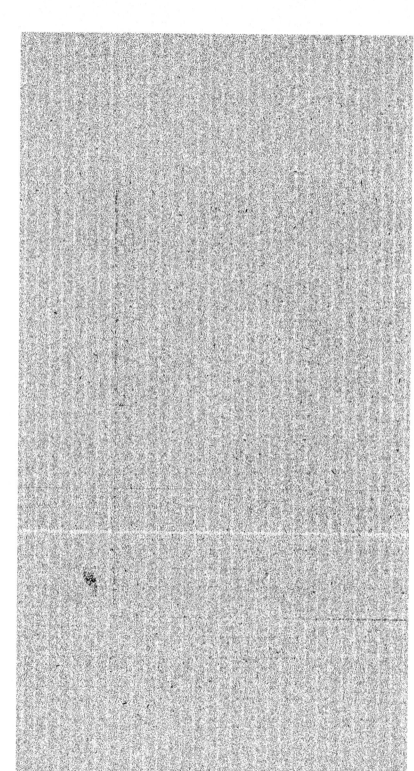

beautiful scene were enchanting; but nothing exceeded the charm of our reception by a host whose graceful mind and manners were unmatched.

The town of Brussels at that time seemed to me rich and lively. In high society, for instance, pleasure was so rife that several friends of the Prince de Ligne would sometimes leave Brussels after breakfast, arrive in Paris for the raising of the curtain at the show, and return to Brussels immediately after, travelling all night. That is what one may call being fond of the Opéra.

We left Brussels for Holland. The sight of Sardam and Mars [1] gave me much pleasure. These two little towns are so clean and well kept that one regards the inhabitants with envy. The streets are very narrow and bordered with canals. Horses take the place of carriages, while little boats are used for the transport of goods. The houses are very low and have two doors: the door of birth and the door of death, through which no one passes except in a coffin. The roofs of these houses shine like steel, while everything is so wonderfully well looked after that I remember seeing outside a farrier's shop a sort of lantern burnished bright enough for a drawing-room.

The women of the people in that part of Holland seemed to me very beautiful, but so timid that the sight of a stranger made them flee. They were so in those days, though I suppose that the presence of Frenchmen in their country may have tamed them.

[1] The author probably refers to the Isle of Marken.

We ended by visiting Amsterdam, where at the Town Hall I saw the superb picture of the burgomasters by Wanols (Vander Helst). I do not think there is any painting more beautiful and true : it is Nature herself. The burgomasters are dressed in black, their 'heads, hands, and draperies being of an inimitable beauty. Those men are alive : one feels one is with them. I am convinced it is the most perfect picture of its kind. I could not cease looking at it. The impression it made upon me keeps it ever before me.

We returned to Flanders to see the masterpieces of Rubens. They were then much better placed than later on in the Paris Museum. In the Flemish churches they all produced an admirable effect. Other masterpieces of this painter adorned private galleries. At Antwerp I saw the famous *Straw Hat* painting which was lately sold to an Englishman for a large sum. It represents one of Rubens' wives. Its chief effect consists in the difference of light between simple daylight and sunshine, though perhaps one must be a painter in order to appreciate Rubens' power of execution. I was so delighted with the picture that it inspired me to paint my own portrait at Brussels in trying to get the same effect. I painted myself wearing a straw hat, a feather and a garland of wild flowers, and holding my palette in my hand. When the portrait was exhibited at the Salon, it added much to my reputation, I venture to say. It was engraved by the celebrated Muller. You must realize, however, that the dark shades of the

64

After my marriage I still lived in the Rue de
Cléry, where M. Le Brun had a large and well-
furnished apartment, in which he placed his pictures
by all the great masters. As for myself, I was
reduced to occupying a little ante-chamber and
a bedroom which served me for a salon. It
was hung with wallpaper similar to the *toile de
Jouy* of my bed-curtains. The furniture was
very simple, perhaps too simple This fact, however, did not prevent M. de Champcenetz (whose
mother-in-law was jealous of me) from writing
that "Mme Le Brun had gilt wainscotings,
lighted her fire with bank-notes, and burnt nothing
but aloe for wood." But I will delay as much
as possible, dear friend, to tell you of the hundreds
of slanders of which I was the victim: we will
return to that subject later on. The reason for
these slanders is to be found in the fact of my
receiving the town and Court every evening in
the modest apartment I have mentioned. Grand
ladies, grand gentlemen, outstanding men of
letters and art—everybody came to that room.
People vied with one another to be invited to
my receptions, where the crowd was often so big
that the marshals of France sat on the floor for
want of a seat, and I remember that the Maréchal
de Noailles, who was very fat and old, was hard
put to it to get up again. I was far from fancying
to myself that everybody came for my sake. As
happens in open houses, the ones came to see the
others, while the greater number came to hear
the best music in Paris. The famous composers,

67

Grétry, Martini, Sacchini, often carried out part
of their operas at my house before their firs
performance. Our usual singers were Garat
Azevédo, Richer, Mme Todi, my sister-in-law
who had a very beautiful voice and could accom
pany at sight, which was very useful to us. Some
times I sang myself, without method, it is true
for I never had time to take lessons, but my voic
was pleasant enough. Grétry said I had silve
tones. Anyhow, it was useless to make any claim
as a singer in the presence of those I have men
tioned. Garat, above all, had the most extra
ordinary talent. Not only did no difficulty exis
for such a flexible throat, but he was also unrivallec
for expression, while no one, in my opinion, ha
sung Gluck so well as he. As for Mme Todi
she possessed a wonderful voice together with al
the qualities of a great cantatrice, singing seriou
and comic works with the same perfection.

For instrumental music I had Viotti the violinist,
whose ravishing play was so full of grace, force-
fulness and expression. Further, Jarnovick, Maes-
trino, Prince Henry of Prussia, an excellent
amateur, who also brought me his first violin.
Salentin played the hautbois, Hulmandel and
Cramer the piano. Mme de Montgeroult also
came once, a short while after her marriage.
Although she was then very young, she astonished
all my very critical company with her admirable
execution and expression. She made the keys
speak. Having risen to the foremost rank as a
pianist, Mme de Montgeroult gained distinction

68

also as a composer. In the days when I gave my concerts, one had both taste and leisure for amusement. Even several years before, the love of music was so general that it gave rise to serious quarrels between the Gluckists and Piccinists.

All music-lovers were divided into two opposing factions. The usual battle-field was the garden of the Palais Royal. There the partisans of Gluck and those of Piccini quarrelled so violently that many a duel was the result. Quarrels also took place in several salons on account of these great masters. Marmontel and the Abbé Arnault were opposed to each other, Marmontel being a Piccinist and the Abbé an ardent Gluckist. Each hurled epigrams and couplets against the other. The Abbé Arnault, for instance, composed the following verses :

> Ce Marmontel, si lent, si lourd,
> Qui ne parle pas, mais qui beugle,
> Juge la peinture en aveugle,
> Et la musique comme un sourd.[1]

Marmontel replied with this couplet :

> L'Abbé Fatras,
> De Carpentras,
> Demande un bénéfice.
> Il l'obtiendra
> Car l'Opéra
> Lui tient lieu d'office.[2]

[1] " This slow, heavy Marmontel, who does not speak, but bellows, judges painting like a blind man, and music like a deaf man."
[2] " The Abbé Fatras of Carpentras asks for a living. He'll get it, for the Opéra serves him instead of the divine office."

69

You will agree, my dear, that the times must have been very happy when people's quarrels were about no graver subjects than those, which could only occur among enlightened folk. But I return to the subject of my concerts.

The women who usually attended them were the Marquise de Groslier, Mme de Verdun, the Marquise de Sabran, who later married the Chevalier de Boufflers, Mme Le Couteulx du Molay, all four my best friends, the Countess de Ségur, the Marquise de Rougé, Mme de Pezé, her friend, whom I painted in the same picture with her, a host of other French ladies whom I could only receive occasionally owing to the smallness of the premises, and the most distinguished foreign ladies. As for the men, the number would be too long to relate in detail, since I believe I received all that Paris could offer in the way of people of talent and wit.

From among this crowd I chose the most agreeable for my invitations to supper, which the Abbé Delille, Lebrun the poet, the Chevalier de Boufflers, the Vicomte de Ségur, and others, made the most amusing in Paris.

It is impossible to realize what French society was like, unless one knows the time when, having finished the business of the day, twelve or fifteen pleasant people would come together at the house of a hostess in order to end their evening. The ease and gentle mirth which prevailed at those light evening meals lent them a charm which dinners will never have. A sort of mutual confidence

GLUCK.

From the painting by Duplessis.

To face p. 71.

and intimacy prevailed among the guests ; and since well-bred people are never troubled with shyness, it was at these suppers that the high society of Paris showed itself superior to the rest of Europe.

At my house, for instance, people came together about nine o'clock. No one ever spoke of politics ; the conversation turned on literature and one told the anecdote of the day. Sometimes we played charades, while at others the Abbé Delille or Lebrun (Pindare) would read his verses to us. At ten o'clock one sat down at table. My supper was of the simplest kind. It consisted of a fowl, a fish, a plate of vegetables and a salad, so that if I ventured to make some visitors stay on for supper, there was really not enough to eat for everybody. That, however, mattered little : everyone was merry and pleasant : hours went by like minutes, till about midnight everyone withdrew.

Apart from the suppers at my house, I often went out to supper, for I was not at leisure till the evening. It was then very pleasant for me to find rest from my work in some pleasant dis- traction. Sometimes it took the shape of a ball, where one was not suffocated as nowadays. Eight persons only formed the set-dance, while the women who did not dance could at least watch the others do so, for the men stood up behind them. Never having any fondness for dancing, I much preferred houses where music was offered. I often spent the evening at the house of M. de

Rivière, where we acted comedy and comic opera. His daughter, my sister-in-law, sang marvellously, and was an excellent actress. M. de Riviére's eldest son was charming in comic parts, while I was given the rôle of lady's maid in opera and comedy. Mme de la Ruette, who had retired from the stage some years previously, did not despise our troupe. She acted with us in several operas, her voice being still very fresh and beautiful. My brother Vigée took the leading parts with great success. Indeed, all our actors were excellent except Talma. Does that make you laugh? The fact is that Talma, who played the lover in our pieces, was awkward and ill at ease, while nobody at the time could have foreseen that he would become an inimitable actor. I admit my surprise was very great when I saw our young actor surpass Larive and replace Lekain. But the time it took to effect this change, as all others of the kind, proves that the dramatic talent is of all talents that which takes the longest to be acquired. Observe that there is not a single great actor known, who was such in his youth.

This letter is enormous. I have no space left to tell you of a certain Grecian supper, which, owing to stupid gossip, was bruited abroad even as far as St. Petersburg. I end with my love to you.

CHAPTER VII

I WILL NOW GIVE YOU, my dear friend,
the exact account of the most brilliant supper
I ever gave in the days when people were
always talking about my luxurious and magnificent
mode of life.

One afternoon, while taking my rest before
receiving a dozen or so persons I had invited,
I got my brother to read aloud to me several
pages of the *Travels of Anarcharsis*. When he
came to the passage describing the way to make
several Grecian sauces, he suggested that I should
have them prepared for table that evening. I
sent immediately for my cook and gave her the
necessary instructions for the preparation of a
certain sauce for the fowl and of another for the
eel. As I was expecting some very beautiful
women, I thought it a good idea to dress everybody in Grecian costumes, in order to have a
surprise ready for M. de Vaudreuil and M. Boutin,
who were not expected till ten o'clock.

My atelier was full of draperies used for my
models, so I hoped to get dresses enough from

that source, while Count de Paroy, who occupied my house in the Rue de Cléry, had a fine collection of Etruscan vases. Luckily, he came to see me that very day about four o'clock. I told him about my plan, and he brought me a lot of cups and vases, from which I made a choice. I cleaned them all myself and put them on a bare mahogany table. After that I placed behind the chairs an immense screen, which I took care to hide beneath some drapery, hung from point to point as one sees in Poussin's pictures. A hanging lamp shed a strong light on to the table. Everything, eve the costumes, having been got ready, Mme Chal grin, the charming daughter of Joseph Vernet was the first to arrive. I did her hair and dressed her at once. The next arrival was the beautiful Mme de Bonneuil. Then came Mme Vigée, my sister-in-law, who was not so pretty but had the most lovely eyes in the world. In a trice al' three were transformed into perfect Athenians Lebrun-Pindare arrived. His powdered wig was taken from him and his tresses were undone a the side, after which I fixed on his head the same crown of laurels which I had just used in painting Prince Henry Lubomirski in *Love of Glory* Count de Paroy had a big clean mantle, with which I immediately transformed Pindare into Anacreon. Then came the Marquis de Cubières While a guitar shaped like a gilt lyre was being fetched from his house, I dressed up my sister-in law's brother M. de Riviére, Ginguené, and Chaudet, the famous sculptor.

74

QUEEN MARIE-ANTOINETTE.

From the painting by Madame Le Brun (Musée de Versailles).

To face p. 74.

The hour was getting late and I had had little time to think about myself; but as I always wore a white dress like a tunic (what is called a blouse nowadays) I needed only to put a veil and a chaplet of flowers on my head. I took particular care with my daughter and Mme de Bonneuil, who was as beautiful as an angel. Both were ravishing to the sight, carrying a very light ancient vase and getting ready to serve us with drink. At half-past nine the preparations were completed. When we were all in our places, the effect of the table was so novel and picturesque that we took turns in getting up and going to look at those who remained seated. At ten o'clock we heard the carriage of Count de Vaudreuil and Boutin enter the courtyard, and when these two gentlemen arrived at the dining-room door, they discovered us singing Gluck's chorus, "Le Dieu de Paphos et de Cnide," which M. de Cubières accompanied on his lyre. In all my life I have never seen two faces so much astonished and dumbfounded as those of M. de Vaudreuil and his companion. They were so surprised and charmed that they remained standing a very long time before making up their minds to occupy the places we had reserved for them.

Besides the two dishes I have already told you of, we had a cake made of honey and currants, and two dishes of vegetables. It is true that we drank a bottle of old Cyprus wine which had been given me for a present. That was all the excess. Nevertheless, we remained at table very long while. Lebrun recited several ode of Anacreon which he had translated. I d not believe I have ever spent a more amusin evening.

M. Boutin and M. de Vaudreuil were so de lighted with the evening that they talked abou it to all their acquaintances next day. Som ladies of the Court begged me to repeat the fun I refused for various reasons, whereat several o the ladies took offence. The report soon go abroad that I had spent twenty thousand franc on the entertainment. The King mentioned i jokingly to the Marquis de Cubiéres, who luckil happened to have been one of the company, an convinced His Majesty of the nonsense of such suggestion.

Nevertheless, the cost, which was kept as modes as twenty thousand at Versailles, rose to fort thousand at Rome. At Vienna, Baroness Stro gonoff told me that I had spent sixty thousan on my Grecian supper. At Petersburg it wa settled at last at eighty thousand. And the trut is, it cost me fifteen francs.

The sad part of all this was that these bas falsehoods were spread all over Europe by m own countrymen. The ridiculous slander of whic I have told you was not the only one with whic people tried to torment my life, as may be see from the following verses addressed to me b Lebrun-Pindare in 1789 and which perhaps yo do not know :

THE TRIANON.

To face p. 76.

A MADAME LE BRUN.

Chère Le Brun, la gloire a ses orages ;
L'Envie est là qui guette le talent ;
Tout ce qui plait, tout mérite excellent
Doit de ce monstre essuyer les outrages.
Qui mieux que toi les mérita jamais ?
Un pinceau mâle anime tes portraits.
Non, tu n'est plus femme que l'on renomme :
L'Envie est juste et ses cris obstinés
Et ses serpents contre toi déchainés
Mieux que nos voix te déclarent grand homme.[1]

Leaving aside the poet's exaggeration regarding
ny talent, it is unfortunately true, however, that
ver since my first appearance in society I have
een made the butt of stupidity and malice. At
rst it was said my works were not my own:
1. Ménageot painted my pictures, even my
ortraits. Though so many people who sat for
e could naturally bear witness to the contrary,
his absurd report was spread abroad even till the
me of my reception into the Royal Academy of
ainting. As I was then exhibiting at the Salon
t the same time as the author of *Méléagre*, the
'uth had to be admitted ; for Ménageot, whose
lent and advice I greatly appreciated, had a
ay of painting entirely opposed to my own.[2]

[1] " Dear Le Brun, glory has its storms. Envy lies in wait for talent.
erything pleasant, all excellent merit, has to undergo the outrages of this
nster. Who ever merited them more than thou ? A manly brush gives
to thy portraits. No, thou art not praised because thou art a woman.
vy is just, and its repeated cries and serpents let loose against thee, proclaim
e better than our voices a great man."
[2] Ménageot's pictures are thoroughly well composed and of good historical
le. He excelled in draping his figures. His *Leonard de Vinci mourant*

Though I believe I was the most harmles creature in existence, I was not without enemies Not only did some women dislike me for no being so ugly as themselves, but several painter could not forgive me for being the fashion an getting a higher price for my pictures than the got for theirs. This led to all sorts of thing being said against me, one of which caused m great distress. Just before the Revolution, painted the portrait of M. de Calonne and exhibite it at the Salon of 1785. I had painted tha Minister, seated, to half-way down the legs. Thi caused Mlle Arnoult to remark : " Mme Le Bru has cut off his legs, so that he may not run away. Unfortunately, that witty remark was not th only one occasioned by my picture, and I foun myself subjected to slanders of the most odiou nature. First of all, absurd stories were tol regarding the fee for the portrait. Some asserte that the Minister of Finance had given me a grea number of bonbons called papillotes wrapped i bank-notes. Others made out that I had receive a pie containing a sum big enough to ruin th Treasury. There were, in fact, hundreds of ve sions, the one more ridiculous than the othe The truth is M. de Calonne sent me four thousan francs in a box valued at twenty louis. Sever of the persons who were present when I receive

dans les bras de Francois I is very remarkable, though not up to the quali of *Méléagre*, which has been kept at the Gobelins to be worked in tapestr M. Ménageot was a very handsome man, thoroughly pleasant, keen-witt and gay. He was therefore much sought after in the best society.

78

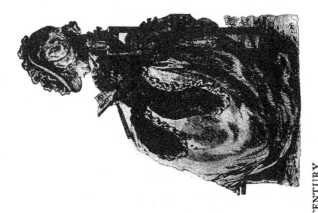

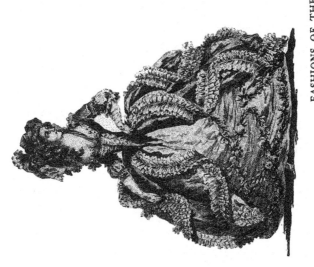

FASHIONS OF THE XVIIIth CENTURY

To face p. 78.

the box are still alive and can testify to the truth of this. Some were even surprised at the meagreness of the sum ; for a short time previously, M. de Beaujon, whom I had painted the same size, had sent me eight thousand francs, which no one took to be an exorbitant price. Nevertheless, the evil-minded set to work to embroider the fact. I was pestered with libels accusing me of living in intimate relationship with M. de Calonne. A certain Gorsas, whom I have never seen or known and who was reported to me as a violent Jacobin, vomited these horrid things against me.

The fact of M. Le Brun having a house built in the Rue du Gros Chenet, though against my desire, served, unfortunately, as a pretext for the calumny. We had, indeed, earned money enough to warrant such an expense. Nevertheless, certain people asserted that M. de Calonne paid for the house.

"See what infamous things are being said," I constantly pointed out to M. Le Brun.—"Let them talk," he replied in gentle anger. "When you are dead, I will raise a pyramid sky-high in my garden and I will have the list of your portraits engraved on it. Then they will know what to think about your fortune." But I confess that the hope of such an honour gave me small consolation for my actual sorrow, which was all the more heartfelt because nobody had feared less than I the possibility of becoming the victim of evil-thinking. I was so careless of money that I was almost unaware of its value. Countess de la Guiche, who is still alive, can relate how she came to ask me to paint her portrait, saying that she could not offer more than a thousand écus ; to which I replied that M. Le Brun did not wish me to paint for less than a hundred louis. This inability to calculate was very unprofitable to me during my last visit to London. I was constantly forgetting that a guinea was worth more than a louis, and in settling the price of my portraits, especially that of Mrs. Canning (in 1803), I reckoned as though I was in Paris.

Moreover, all those who were around me know that M. Le Brun took charge of all my earnings, telling me that he would use them to advantage in his business. Often I kept no more than six francs in my pocket. When I painted the portrait of the handsome Prince Lubomirski in 1788, Princess Lubomirska, his aunt, sent me twelve thousand francs, of which sum I begged M. Le Brun to leave me two louis. He refused, saying that he needed the whole sum in order to settle an account It was more usual, in fact, for M. Le Brun himself to receive the money, and very often he failed to tell I had been paid. Once only in my life, in September 1789, did I receive the fee for a portrait ; that was when the Bailiff of Crussol sent me one hundred lois. Happily, my husband was away, so that I was able to keep the money, which paid for my journey to Rome a few days later (September 5th).

My indifference to money was no doubt at that time due to the little need I had to be rich. My house required no luxury to make it pleasant,

nd I have always lived very modestly. I spent
ery little on clothes. In this respect I was even
ccused of being too careless, for I always wore
hite dresses of muslin or linen, and never had
ny ornamental dresses made except for my sittings
Versailles. My head-gear never cost me any-
ing. I did my own hair-dressing and generally
visted a muslin fichu about my head, as may be
en in my portraits in Florence, St. Petersburg,
nd at M. de Laborde's house in Paris. I painted
yself in this manner in all my portraits except
le one at the Home Office, where I am in a
reek costume.

Certainly, a woman of that sort was not likely
be seduced by the title of Finance Minister,
hile, in every other respect, M. de Calonne
ways seemed to me unattractive, for he wore a
cal wig. A wig! Just imagine me, with my
ndness for the picturesque, being able to put up
th a wig! I have always detested them, so
uch so that I once refused a rich suitor because
wore a wig. I never painted bewigged men
cept with regret.

The surprising part of this affair is that there
s nothing to offer even the shadow of likelihood
slander. I scarcely knew M. de Calonne.
nce only in my life had I been to his abode at
e Ministry of Finance. He was giving a grand
rty for Prince Henry of Prussia, and as the latter
ually visited my house, he had thought it proper
invite me. Moreover, I remember hurrying
portrait to the extent of painting the hands

without his sitting for them, though it was my custom always to paint them from life.

I should never have guessed the source of these distressing reports, had I not discovered later of a truly hellish perfidy.

M. de Calonne used often to go to the Rue du Gros Chenet (I was not living there at the time) to the house of Mme de S——, wife of D—— nicknamed "The Rake." [1] Mme de S—— had a sweet and charming face, although one could notice something false in her look. M. de Calonne was very much in love with her. At the time am speaking of, she had asked me to paint her portrait. One day, while sitting for me, she asked me with her usual sweetness if I would lend her my carriage in order to go to the play that evening. I consented, and my coachman went to her house to get her. Next morning I ordered my carriage for eleven o'clock. At eleven o'clock, however, neither coachman nor carriage had returned. I immediately sent a messenger to Mme de S——'s house. Mme de S—— had not returned at all. She had spent the night at the palace of the Minister of Finance! Judge of my anger when I heard the news a few days later through my coachman, whom a large bribe had failed to keep silent and who had related the matter to several people in the house. Thinking

[1] These are the only names dissimulated by Mme Vigée-Le Brun in her *Memoirs*. They refer to Countess de Serre, wife of Jean Du Barry, the famous "Rake," who called himself Count de Serre at Toulouse. The family lived in Paris in 1785.

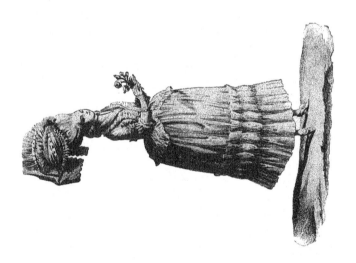

that if the people at the Finance palace or others had asked the coachman the name of his employers he would naturally have answered that it belonged to Mme Le Brun, I was quite beyond myself. It is useless to add that I have never seen Mme de S—— again. I am told she is living at Toulouse, practising the most austere life of religious devotion. May God grant her pardon ! Did she try to save her reputation at the cost of mine? Did she hate me ? I do not know. But she did me great harm, for the long details I have set out, dear friend, prove how much I have suffered from a slander which was so little in keeping with my character and the conduct of a whole lifetime, which I venture to say has been one of honour.

This is truly a sad letter, fit to turn one with disgust from celebrity, especially if one has the misfortune to be a woman. Somebody said to me one day : " When I look at you and think of your fame, I seem to see rays about your head." —" Ah ! " I replied with a sigh. " There may well be a few little serpents among them." And really, has one ever known a great reputation, in whatever matter, that failed to arouse envy ? It is true that it also attracts towards you your most distinguished contemporaries ; and that association makes up for many things. When I think of the great number of pleasant and good people, whose friendship I owe to my talent, I pride myself with having made my name known ; while to put everything in a nutshell, dear friend, when I think of you, I forget the wicked.

ONE OF MY FAVOURITE relaxations was
to go to the playhouse. I can tell yo
that the actors were so brilliant that many
of them have never been equalled. I remember
the celebrated actor Lekain. Though I was ther
too young to appreciate his great talent, the
applause and enthusiasm he aroused told me how
brilliant a tragedian he was. The amazing uglines
of Lekain vanished when he played certain charac
ters. The costume of knight, for instance, softene
so much the stern and repellent expression o
his face, the features of which were irregular
that it was possible to look at it when he playe
Tancrede. I once saw him in the rôle of Orosman
at very close quarters, and the turban made hir
look so hideous that I was filled with drea
although I admired his fine and noble manner.

At the time when Lekain was playing th
principal parts, as well as some time after, I sa
Brizard and Mlle Dumesnil. Brizard acted th

MARIE-ANTOINETTE'S ARRIVAL AT NOTRE-DAME FOR A
THANKSGIVING SERVICE.

To face p. 85.

part of father, nature seeming to have created him for that office. His white hair, imposing figure and superb voice gave him the noblest and most respectable character imaginable. He excelled above all in *King Lear* and in Ducis' *Oedipe*. So grand was the aspect of the man who acted the parts of these two old unfortunate princes that you would have believed you really saw them.

Mlle Dumesnil, though small and very ugly, aroused enthusiasm in the great tragic rôles. Her talent was very unbalanced. She sometimes bordered on triviality, though she had her sublime moments. In general, she was better at expressing fury than affection, unless it was maternal affection, one of her finest parts being that of Mérope. She sometimes played part of a play without making any effect. Then of a sudden she would brighten up, her gestures, voice and looks becoming so wonderfully tragic that she won the applause of the entire theatre. I was told that she always drank a bottle of wine before going on to the stage, and that she always had another kept ready in the side-scenes.

One of the most remarkable actors of the Théâtre Français, in tragedy and comedy, was Monvel. He was prevented from attaining front rank by a few physical defects and the weakness of his voice, but his soul, ardour and perfect delivery were excellent. When I returned to France he had given up playing young leading parts and was acting the part of a noble father. I saw him act Auguste in Cinna and the Abbé de l'Epée most admirably. In the latter rôle he was so real that one day when he greeted the personages of the piece just before leaving the stage, I rose and returned his greeting, which amused very much the people who were with me in the box.

The most brilliant début I ever saw was that of Mlle Raucourt in the rôle of Didon. She could not have been more than eighteen or twenty years old. The beauty of her features, her figure, voice, delivery, all bespoke a perfect actress. To so many advantages she united a most remarkable stateliness and the reputation of an austere staidness that caused her to be much courted by our greatest ladies. She was given jewels, her theatre costumes, as well as money for herself and her father, who was always at her side. Later on she must have changed her mode of life. It is said that the first happy mortal to triumph over so much virtue was the Marquis de Bièvres, and that when she forsook him for another lover he exclaimed : " Ah ! the ungrateful woman has my income ! " Though Mlle Raucourt may not have remained virtuous, she certainly remained a great tragedian. But her voice became so harsh and hard that, listening to her with one's eyes shut, one thought it was a man speaking. Not till her death did she leave the stage, where she ended up by playing the parts of mothers and queens with tremendous success.

Other actresses I saw were the Mlles Sainval and Mme Vestris, the sister of Dugazon. The

MADAME ELIZABETH OF FRANCE.
From a painting by Madame Le Brun (Musée de Versailles).

To face p. 87.

two former were given a little too much to weeping, but both, especially the younger, seemed to me to be greater tragediennes than Mme Vestris, who, in spite of her beauty, never gained any great success, except in the rôle of Gabrielle de Vergy, when, in the last act, she created a heart-rending effect. It must, however, be said that the scene is horrible.

Larive, who had the ill-luck to succeed Lekain, still fresh in people's memories, had more talent than old theatre-goers were willing to grant. It was the comparison alone that did him injustice, for he lacked neither nobility nor energy. His face was handsome. He was big and well made, but never upright on his legs, which led to its being said that he walked beside himself.

Larive had a very good manner and conversed wittily, even on matters unconnected with his art, so that he was always in good company. My brother introduced him to me. Knowing that he was intimately associated with Mlle Clairon, I once remarked to him that I would like to meet that great tragedienne, whom I had never seen on the stage. He immediately begged me to dine at his house in order to bring us together. I accepted the invitation. Two days later I went to the house he had had built for himself in the Gros-Caillou. It was a charming house, appointed in perfect taste, besides having a beautiful garden which offered one the delights of the country in Paris. Larive took me round his arches under climbing vines in the style of the ancients, such as one sees in the neighbourhood of Naples. Just as we returned to the salon for dinner, Mlle Clairon was announced. I had imagined her to be very big. She was, however very small and thin. She carried her head very high, which made her look very dignified. On the other hand, I have never heard anyone speak with so much bombast, for she always kept the tragic tone and the airs of a princess. But she seemed to me well-informed and fine-witted. I sat next to her at table and much enjoyed her conversation. Larive showed a great respect for her, revealing both admiration and gratitude, with which he never ceased talking of her.

On my return to France, I was delighted to see Larive again, meeting him frequently at the house of the Marquise de Grollier at Epinay, Having left the stage, he was then living at a charming country house near by. Mme de Grollier was delighted to have him for a neighbour. He treated us to wonderful readings ; his way of reciting verses was much enhanced by the beauty of his voice.

Talma, our last great tragedian, surpassed all others, in my opinion. His acting was genial. Moreover, he may be said to have revolutionize the art, first of all, by doing away with the bombastic, affected manner of reciting, and by his natural and true delivery ; secondly, by changing the style of the costumes, for he dressed as a Greek and Roman when acting the parts of Achilles and Brutus. Talma had a very fine head and

88

ne of the most flexible faces ever seen. Howver fiery his acting became, he always remained oble, which is, I think, the first quality in a ragedian. His voice was at times rather damped. t was more suited to furious or deep parts rather han brilliant ones. For this reason he was specially admirable in the rôles of Areste and anlius, but he had several sublime moments in ll. The last rôle he thought out has never since een played. I do not believe anyone would are, for Talma showed himself therein superior ɔ himself. It was no longer an actor; it was harles VI himself, an unhappy king, an unhappy ool in all his frightful truth. Alas! death folowed so closely on his triumph. What Paris ad applauded so enthusiastically was the deathong of the swan.

Talma was an excellent man, the easiest of all o get along with. He was generally very little rouble in society, an interesting word in the onversation being all that was necessary to animate him. He would then become very interesting to isten to, especially when he talked of his art.

Comedy was perhaps richer in talents than ragedy. I often had the pleasure of seeing Préille act. What a perfect, inimitable actor! His cting was full of wit, good-nature and gaiety, besides being most varied. If he played Crispin, Sosie, Figaro, one after the other, you would not recognize the same man, so inexhaustible were the shades in his interpretation of the comical. For this reason he has never been replaced. He was so naturally genuine that all his imitators had only succeeded in showing his superiority. I make no exception of Dugazon, who certainly had great talent, but as Figaro in the *Barber of Seville*, for instance, he never came up to his model.

I dined with Préville several times. It was a rare thing to meet so pleasant a companion at table. His witty merriment charmed every one of us. He was very clever at telling anecdotes of an extremely piquant nature. People sought eagerly for the chance of being together with him.

Dugazon, his successor in comic rules, would have made an excellent comedian if the desire to make the public laugh had not led him pretty often into farce. He was very good in certain parts as valet. He had a biting manner, a perfect expression, and might have equalled Préville if he had avoided exaggeration. One is induced to believe that his nature led him to choose that wretched style by the fact that the shade of difference on the stage between him and his predecessor was evident in the salons as well. In the latter, Préville was always a pleasant man, while Dugazon was a very witty buffoon. He was therefore only received occasionally in order to amuse the guests. He was, indeed, very entertaining, especially after dinner. His conduct in the Revolution was atrocious. He was one of those who went to fetch the King at Varennes, while an eye-witness related to me how he had seen him at the door of the carriage with a gun on his shoulder. All this in spite of the fact o

THE MUSIC LESSON.

After Moreau, junior.

To face p. 90

is having been overwhelmed with favours by
he Court, especially by the Count d'Artois.

I remember seeing Mlle Doligny in young
eading parts, which she acted to perfection. She
was so natural, witty and good that her great
talent made one forget her ugliness. I also saw
he début of Mlle Contat. She was extremely
pretty and well made, but acted so badly at first
that nobody expected she would become so
excellent an actress. Her charming face was not
always sufficient to keep her from being hissed,
when Beaumarchais gave her the part of Suzanne
in the *Marriage of Figaro*. From that time on-
wards she had one success after another, in the
role of grande coquette at first, then in parts more
suitable to her age and particularly her figure,
which, unfortunately, had grown too plump. Mlle
Contat married M. de Parny, a nephew of the
poet of that name, but the marriage was not
announced until after she had left the theatre.
Her face remained attractive until her death. I
have never seen a more bewitching smile. Her
great wit rendered her conversation very spicy,
while she seemed to me so pleasant that I often
invited her to my house.

Mlle Contat was admirably seconded in all her
roles by Molé, who almost always acted with
her. Though never the equal of Préville, Molé
was a great actor. He had both grace and dignity
and filled the stage, so to speak. Moreover, I
have seldom seen so varied and brilliant a talent
as his. I received him at my house several times.

Though his acting was very fine, Molé had n
outstanding social gifts excepting a very goo
manner.

Fleury, who succeeded him in the foremc
rôles, was the last to maintain the tradition
high comedy. He had less lyricism and sublimi
of style than Molé, but he surpassed all othe
in portraying young grand gentlemen. As
was very witty and well-mannered, he mixe
with high society and assimilated so well
customs, charms and whims that a few years ag
he still offered us a perfect copy of models th
have died out.

When all the great actors I have mentione
began to grow old, there arose a young tale
who is the ornament of the French stage to-da
Mlle Mars was inimitable in playing the part
the Ingénue. She excelled in that of Victori
in *Philosophe sans le Savoir*, and in a score
others in which no one else has been able to ta
her place, for it is impossible to be so lifeli
and moving. She was indeed nature itself wi
all its charm. When you saw Mlle Mars, n
dear friend, she had already taken the place
Mlle Contat, whom she alone was able to eclips
No doubt you remember her pretty face, fi
figure and angelic voice. Fortunately they ha
all been so well preserved that Mlle Mars has
age at all, and never will have, I believe. T
enthusiasm of the public every evening prov
that it shares my opinion. I remember twi
seeing Mlle Arnoult act in *Castor et Pollux*

MADAME DU BARRY'S PAVILION AT LOUVECIENNES.

To face p. 92.

e Grand Opéra. I was then hardly able to
dge of her talent as an actress. I remember,
wever, that she seemed to me to have both
ace and the power of expression. As for her
lent as a singer, I was so horribly bored by the
usic of those days that I listened too badly to
˻ able to speak about it. Mlle Arnoult was
ot at all pretty ; her mouth was out of keeping
ith her face, her eyes alone imparting an expres-
on in which resided the remarkable spirit that
as made her famous. Many anécdotes about
er have been told and printed. Here is one
hich I do not think is known and which I find
ery comical : She was attending the marriage
f her daughter together with the bridegroom's
other, aunt, and several female relations. During
he wedding rite, Mlle Arnoult turned round
nd said to them : " How nice ! I am the only
irl here ! "
  Mlle Arnoult was succeeded by a woman whose
utstanding talent delighted us a long while.
he was Mme Saint-Hubert, who had to be
eard in order to realize what heights lyrical
agedy can reach. Not only did she possess a
lorious voice, but she was also a great actress.
 was her good fortune to have to sing to the
peras of Piccini, Sacchini, and Gluck, whose
eautiful and expressive music thoroughly suited
er talent, which was full of expression, faithfulness
 life and nobility. It is impossible to be more
ffecting than she was in the rôles of Alceste,
)idon, etc. She was ˻ always so genuine and

noble, that her song drew tears from the whol theatre. I still remember certain words and note which it was impossible to resist.

Mme Saint-Hubert was not pretty, but sh had a charming expression. Count d'Entraigues, a very handsome man, much distinguished for his wit, fell so much in love with her that he married her. When the Revolution broke out he took refuge with her in London. It was there that they were both assassinated one evening as they were getting into a carriage. Neither the assassins nor the motives for such a wicked crime were ever discovered.

As far as singing was concerned, the entire Opéra held nobody but Mme Saint-Hubert for me, so I will not talk of those who sang with her. I could hardly listen to them. I preferred to keep part of my attention for the ballets, in which several remarkable talents were appearing. Gardel and Vestris *père* held the front rank. I often saw them dancing together, especially in a Spanish dance in one of Grétry's operas, which attracted all Paris. It was a *pas de deux* in which the two dancers pursued Mlle Guimard, who was very small and thin. On this account they were likened to two big dogs quarrelling over a bone. Gardel always seemed to me to be much inferior to Vestris *père*, who was a big, handsome man, dancing solemn, stately dances to perfection. I am at a loss to describe the consummate grace with which he doffed and replaced his hat when performing the greeting that preceded the minuet.

94

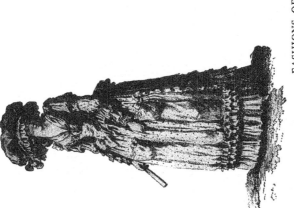

FASHIONS OF THE XVIIIth CENTURY.

To face p. 94.

In fact, all the young débutantes at the Court took him as a model in learning how to make their three curtseys.

Vestris *père* was succeeded by his son, the most surprising dancer ever seen, so great were his grace and lightness. Although our modern dancers do not stint the number of their pirouettes, none of them will ever make as many as he did. He would suddenly spring into the air in so amazing a manner that you thought he had wings. This led Vestris *père* to say : " If my son touches the ground, he does so by way of procedure for the sake of his colleagues."

Mlle Pélin and Mlle Allard were two dancers in what is called the grotesque style in Italy. They did stunts, endless pirouettes without any charm. Both of them, however, though very stout, possessed an astonishing agility, especially Mlle Allard.

Mlle Guimard's talent was altogether different. Her dance was a mere sketch. She danced nothing but small steps, though with such graceful movements that the public preferred her to all other dancers. She was small, slim and shapely, and although ugly, had such fine features that even at the age of forty-five she seemed on the stage to be no more than fifteen.

A happy rival to the Grand Opéra was the Opéra Comique, which I saw constructed. It took the place of what was called the Italian Comedy. It would be hard for me to tell you anything about the latter, if I did not remember

95

having been there to see Carlin. Though very young at the time, I still retain a memory of him. Carlin acted Harlequin in sketches, a sort of proverbs, which required witty actors. His flashes of wit were inexhaustible, the spontaneity and brightness of his acting making him an exceptional actor. Though very stout, he was very nimble in his movements. I was told that he studied his graceful gestures by watching kittens at play. He certainly had their suppleness. His appearance alone was sufficient to draw the public, fill the theatre and charm the spectators. When he disappeared, the Italian Comedy came to an end.

The lyrical company which took his place was very talented and sang the operas of Duni, Philidor and Grétry, etc. The public loved Caillot above all. He left the theatre when I was still very young. Nevertheless, twice I saw him act in *Annette et Lubin.* His handsome looks and glorious voice would have remained in my memory even though I had not had the pleasure later of of acting in comedy with him in society. During one of his greatest successes on the stage a slight accident happened to his throat, as sometimes happens with the best of singers. Somebody in the audience hissed, and Caillot was so deeply offended that he abandoned the stage from that evening, and neither prayers nor supplications have induced him to appear in public since.

Besides his great talent, Caillot had plenty of wit. He was very charming in society, where

96

open-hearted gaiety created an atmosphere of
yfulness. He was a wonderful story-teller. At
unt de Vaudreuil's at Gennevilliers he was the
urce of great amusement at table and in the
on, where he would relate a spicy anecdote or
g to us in his beautiful voice the romances
d ditties of the day. As he was a great sports-
an, he was always invited to the shooting parties.
unt de Vaudreuil, with whom he was always on
endly terms, induced the Count d'Artois to
ve him a little pavilion called Le Belloi, that
is situated at the end of the terrace at Saint
ermain and had a very pretty garden.

There, Caillot lived in great happiness with his
fe and children. I stayed at his house several
ys, when his happiness reminded me of Lubin,
nose rôle I had often seen him perform. In
ving him the pavilion, the Count d'Artois
d named him captain of the hunt of the whole
strict. He wore the uniform of this office, and
was in that dress that I painted him carrying
s gun on his shoulder. His handsome, laughing
oks inspired me so much that I finished the
ortrait in one sitting

When the Revolution came, Caillot fell under
ave suspicion because he had received favours
om a prince. I was told, though I refuse to
lieve, that he proved to be a thankless man
d behaved like a Jacobin. If the story is true,
am convinced that fear and his wife turned his
ain. I have reasons for believing that his wife
is an ardent revolutionary. When I was in

G   97

Rome in 1791, I received a letter from her urging
me to return to France, and telling me that w
should all be equal and that it would be th
golden age. Fortunately I did not believe her
for one knows what sort of golden age it wa
that followed. Shortly after receiving this lette
I learnt that Mme Caillot had thrown herself ou
of a window in despair.

Laruette and his wife remained on the stage
longer than Caillot. They were both perfect i
their style. Mme Laruette especially acted in
charming manner with much ingenuity, and sang
with inimitable taste and expression. Though
more than fifty years old, she looked no more
than sixteen, her figure being so young and he
features delicate. Not only did she avoid th
ridiculous in acting naïve persons, but made them
charming. Perhaps the enthusiasm and regrets of
the public were never so strong as on the day
she left the stage, when she acted for the last
time the two young parts in *Isabelle et Gertrude*
and in some other opera. Though I saw her act
very rarely, I still remember her perfectly.

I come at last to the actress whose dramati
career I was able to follow in its entirety. This
was Mme Dugazon, the most perfect talent tha
the Opéra Comique has ever possessed.

Never has such truthfulness been seen on th
stage. Mme Dugazon was one of those born
talents who seem to owe nothing to study. One
was unconscious of the actress. One was aware
only of Babet, Countess d'Albert or Nicolette

oble, naïve, graceful, spicy, she had a score of
spects, making her accents suit the person. Her
oice was rather weak, but it was sufficient for
ears and laughter, for all situations and rôles.
rétry and Dalayrac, who worked with her, were
ad about her, and I, too, was mad.

The latter word reminds me of a rôle in which
many vain attempts have been made to copy her.
Nobody has ever been able to give us back Nina,
Nina at once so sedate and passionate, so unhappy
and touching, the mere sight of her drew tears
from the spectators. I believe I saw Nina twenty
times at least, and each time my emotion was the
same. I was too much thrilled by Mme Dugazon
not to invite her often to supper at my house.
We noticed that after playing Nina she still kept
her eyes rather haggard, so that she remained
Nina all the evening. To this power of steeping
herself so thoroughly in her rôle is due, no doubt,
the astounding perfection of her talent.

Mme Dugazon was a royalist in heart and soul.
This she proved to the public one evening long
fter the outbreak of the Revolution, when she
was taking the part of lady's maid in *Evénements
Imprévus*. The Queen was present at the performance. In a duet which the valet begins with
he words " I love my master tenderly," Mme
Dugazon, whose reply was, " Ah, as I love my
mistress," turned to Her Majesty's box and sang
her lines with great emotion, while bowing towards
he Queen. I was told that shortly afterwards
he public (and what a public !) wanted to take

its revenge for that noble action by insisting on her singing some dreadful thing which used to be sung on the stage every evening. Mme Dugazon would not yield, but left the stage.

The unusual length of this letter proves, my dear friend, how much I loved acting in comedy myself, for I have spared you no details. Adieu.

"IT'S A SON, MONSIEUR!"

After Moreau, junior (1776).

To face p 101.

CHAPTER IX

TO MY GREAT REGRET, I was unable to stay in the country for any length of time, but I never missed a chance of passing a few days there. I was invited to stay at some of the finest places in the neighbourhood of Paris. I saw the magnificent fêtes at Chantilly, organized and presided over by the Prince de Condé, who returned to France with Louis XVIII. You know the splendid Château de Chantilly. Its immense gallery was then adorned with French armoury of different centuries, some of the pieces being so enormous and heavy that they seemed to have been made for giants. It was, I think, a suitable decoration for the house of a descendant of the great Condé. At the end of the gallery was the mask of Henri IV, taken immediately after his death and still showing a few hairs of the good King's eyebrows. I do not know what became of this mask, which was reproduced a good deal in plaster. As for the armoury, it was pillaged during the Revolution and part of it is now in a museum.

The château had a certain grandeur, which made it worthy of its owners. The dining-room was very beautiful, having marble columns, between which were large marble basins that received cascades of limpid and constantly changing water. The room seemed to be in the open air and looked quite magical. The immense park put one in mind of fairyland with its lakes and flower-bordered streams. The hamlet was charming, its cottages having interiors that sparkled with the greatest magnificence. Everything, indeed, made Chantilly a wonderful abode. Strangers went there in crowds in the happy days I am talking of, when the master of that beautiful place lived there amidst the devoted inhabitants, who were overwhelmed with his favours and have deeply regretted him ever since.

In 1782 I stayed a short time at Raincy, having been invited there by the Duke of Orleans in order to paint his portrait and that of Mme de Montesson. With the exception of the pleasure I took in joining the shooting parties, I spent a rather dull time there. After my sittings, I had no agreeable society apart from that of Mme Berthollet, a very pleasant woman, who played the harp beautifully. Saint-Georges, the clever, muscular mulatto, was one of the shooting party. It was there that I realized how some men, especially princes, get passionately fond of shooting. When many people are gathered together, it is an exercise that provides a really fine spectacle. The general fussing about, together with the

THE COMTE DE PROVENCE.

To face p. 1

sound of the horns, is truly something war-like.

Talking of this trip, I cannot recall without laughing a certain incident that shocked me a good deal at the time. While I was painting Mme de Montesson, the old Princess de Conti came one day on a visit. This Princess always called me " mademoiselle." It is true that once upon a time great ladies always addressed their inferiors in this way. But this disdainful Court manner had gone out of fashion with Louis XV. I was then about to go to bed with my first child, which made the matter altogether odd.

If my trip to Raincy was not very gay, I cannot say the same of my visits to Gennevilliers, which then belonged to Count de Vaudreuil, one of the most agreeable men in existence. Gennevilliers was in no way picturesque. Count de Vaudreuil had bought the place largely on behalf of the Count d'Artois, because it contained some fine shooting districts, and he had adorned it as well as he could.

The house was furnished in the best taste, though without any magnificence. It had a small but charming acting-room, in which my sister-in-law, my brother, M. de Rivière and I per-formed several comic operas with Mme Dugazon, Garat, Caillot and Laruette.

The two last, who had retired from the stage, acted wonderfully and with such simplicity that one day when they were rehearsing the scene of the two fathers in *Rose et Colas*, I thought they were talking together, and I said to them : " Come, let's begin the rehearsal."

I was given the part of Rose. Garat acted that of Colas rather awkwardly, but his singing was so wonderful ! He was delightful to hear in *La Colonie*, especially, the music of which is ravishing, in my opinion.

He took the part of Saint-Albe, while I took the rôle of Marine, and my sister-in-law that of the countess, which she played like an angel. She and M. de Riviére were real actors ; they would have shone on the stage.

The Count d'Artois and his society came to witness our performances.

I confess that I was so afraid of all these fine people the first time they came without my having been warned, that I did not wish to act. It was only through fear of disappointing the friends who were to act with me that I decided to appear on the stage. And the Count d'Artois, with his usual grace, came in the interval between the two plays to encourage us with all sorts of compliments.

The last performance given in the acting-room at Gennevilliers was that of the *Marriage of Figaro* by the actors of the Comédie Française. I remember Mlle Sainval took the part of the countess, Mlle Olivier that of the page, while Mlle Contat was charming in the rôle of Suzanne. Beaumarchais, however, must have worried M. de Vaudreuil enormously to succeed in having such an inconvenient piece performed in that

104

heatre. Dialogue and couplets, the whole piece in fact, was directed against the Court, of which great part was present, not to mention our excellent Prince. Everybody felt the inconvenience of such a lack of taste. Beaumarchais, however, was none the less overwhelmed with satisfaction, running about like a man beside himself. When a complaint was made about the heat, he did not give one time to open the windows, but smashed all the panes with his walking-stick; which led to its being said, after the performance, that he had smashed the windows in more than one sense.

Count de Vaudreuil had also to regret in more than one sense having given his patronage to the author of the *Marriage of Figaro*.

Shortly after the performance in question, Beaumarchais begged him for an interview. His request was granted immediately, and he arrived at Versailles so early that the Count had scarcely got out of bed. He then spoke of a financial project he had thought out and which was expected to bring him much profit. Finally he offered Count de Vaudreuil a considerable sum if he would consent to assist in realizing the project. The Count listened to him with the utmost calm. When Beaumarchais had finished talking, the Count said to him : " Monsieur de Beaumarchais, you could not have come at a more favourable moment, for I have spent a good night, had a good digestion, and never felt so well as I do to-day. If you had made such a proposal to me yesterday, I would have had you thrown out of the window."

One of the beautiful country places I saw wa Villette. The Marquise de Villette, " Belle e Bonne," having invited me to visit her there, went and stayed several days. Among my paper I find some very pretty verses which M. d Villette wrote on the occasion of my arrival. copy them here and beg you not to forget tha it is a poet who speaks :

> J'avais lu dans les vieux auteurs
> Que les dieux autrefois visitaient les pasterus,
> Et qu'ils venaient charmer leur belle solitude :
> J'amais me bercer de ces douces erreurs.
> Embellir ces forêts devint ma seule étude,
> J'y créai des jardins, je les semai de fleurs ;
> Mais des dieux vainement j'attendais la présence.
> O sublime Le Brun ! vous, l'orgueil de la France,
> Dont l'esprit créateur, dont l'immortel crayon
> De plaire et d'étonner a la double puissance
> Et fait naitre l'amour par l'admiration,
>> La gloire qui vous accompagne
>> Aggrandit ce petit château ;
>> Elle ranime la campagne ;
>> Vous nous rendez le jour plus beau,
>> Et vous réalisez mes châteaux en Espagne.[1]

[1] " I had read in old authors that the gods once used to visit shepher in order to give delight to their solitude. I loved to cherish these sweet erro It was my one aim to embellish these forests. I created gardens there a sowed them with flowers. But I waited in vain for the gods to come. C sublime Le Brun ! you, the pride of France, whose creative spirit and immor pencil had power both to please and astonish, and to make love spring fro admiration, the glory that accompanies you, increases the size of this lit château and enlivens the country. You make the day more beautiful for and realize my castles in Spain."

Once we found in the park a man who was
ainting the fences. This dauber was so efficient
at M. de Villette complimented him.

" Me ! " the man replied. " I make a point of
otting out in a day what Rubens painted in a
fetime."

Mme de Villette was a very graceful hostess.
he was, above all, extremely benevolent. In her
ark I saw a round, natural hillock where she
as said to gather the village maidens and teach
em like a schoolmaster.

Ah ! how I would have loved to go for walks
ith you in the wood at Moulin Joli ! It was
he of those places one never forgets, so beautiful,
varied, picturesque, Elysian, wild, ravishing !
magine a large island covered with woods, gardens
d orchards, cut through the middle by the
ine. The shores were connected by a bridge
f boats, decorated along the sides with boxes of
wers, while seats placed at intervals allowed
e to enjoy the balmy air and wonderful
ews a long while. The bridge, seen from afar
th its reflection in the water, had a most charming
fect. Lofty trees of sturdy aspect lined the
ght shore, while the left was covered with
ormous poplars and weeping-willows, whose
nder green branches reached down to the water
e bowers. One of these willows formed a
rge vault beneath which one could rest or dream
lightfully. Words fail to express the happiness
felt in that delightful spot, with which I have
ver seen anything to be compared.

This Elysian place belonged to an acquaintan of mine, M. Watelet, a great lover of the ai and the author of a poem on painting. He w a very distinguished man, of an attractive di position, who had a good number of frienc On his enchanted island I found him in keepir with all his surroundings. There he graceful received a small but very well-chosen compan A friend (Marguerite Lecomte), to whom he ha been attached over thirty years, was established his house, time having, so to speak, sanctifie their relationship, so that they were received . the best society, together with the lady's husban who, strange to say, never left her.

Later on, in 1788, Moulin Joli was bought l a certain M. Gaudran, a wealthy merchant, wl invited me and my family to stay a month ther The new owner had no idea of what was picturesqu and I was sorry to see that he had already spo some parts of that Elysian place. Happily tl chief beauties had remained intact. Robert, tl landscape painter, and I found all the enchantmei of the place once again. During the visit question I painted one of my best portraits, th of Robert, with my palette in my hand. Lebru Pindare composed his *Exegi Monumentum,* a prou piece justified by its beauty. My brother al wrote some very pretty verses. Those woo inspired all of us. M. de Calonne, who ga me so many things, as you are aware, is said have given me Moulin Joli as well. Ah ! if had had Moulin Joli, I would never have left

108

[y great regret, however, is not to have bought
on my return to France, when it was for sale.
was prevented from buying it through the
elay of some funds I was expecting from Russia.
was sold for eighty thousand francs to a copper-
mith, who recovered his outlay by cutting down
ll the beautiful trees. And now, when my
memory takes me back to that delightful place, I
m filled with the sad thought of its complete
estruction.

Shortly before the Revolution I went to Mor-
ontaine, and from there we made a trip to
rmenonville, where I saw the tomb of J. J.
Rousseau. The fame of the beautiful park of
rmenonville spoilt the pleasure of the trip for
e. There were inscriptions at almost every step—
veritable tyranny over the mind.

At Morfontaine I always preferred the picturesque part of the park which is not set out
n the English way, where there is now a great
ake. All artists accord it the front rank in its
nd. At the time I mention, M. de Morfontaine
ad adorned it with canals, on which we used to
o boating. The lake was not then so large,
nd was divided by charming islands. At present
ere is only one small island, which looks to me
ke a piece of pastry in the middle of that immense
retch of water.

M. de Morfontaine received his visitors with
ch unaffected kindness that they felt quite at
ome. Count de Vaudreuil, Lebrun the poet,
e Chevalier de Coigny, so amiable and gay,

Brogniart, Robert, Rivière and my brother, playe
charades every night and woke one another u
to tell them. This foolish gaiety proves ho
great was the freedom one enjoyed in that beautif
place. In truth, order was banished from it
well as awkwardness. Happily we were all in
mate friends and few in number, for I have nev
seen a house-party so ill-behaved. M. de Mo
fontaine carried the Bohemianism to an unimagi
able degree, and you can realize how much h
house was affected by such a mode of living.

In those days M. Le Pelletier de Morfontai
was merchants' provost. He built one of t
bridges of Paris. I remember he used to car
in his pocket a little note-book in which he co
stantly wrote the remarkable things he heard i
society. I often tried to read over his shoulde
but though his letters were very large, I was nev
able to decipher a single word, so shapeless w
his handwriting. I challenge his heirs to mak
head or tail of the memoirs he must have left.

On arriving at Maupertuis after Morfontain
one could not help comparing the two house
The difference was striking. Order and magn
ficence reigned everywhere at Maupertuis. A
the latter place, M. de Montesquiou lived like
great gentleman. Being equerry to Monsie
(later Louis XVIII), he had no difficulty in puttin
at our disposal horses, calèches and carriages
every sort. The meals were splendid. Th
château was large enough to accommodate thir
or forty households, all well lodged and cared fo

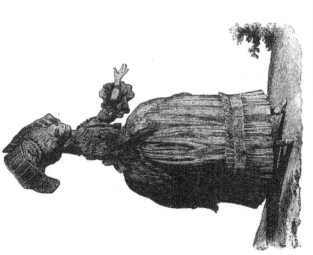

FASHIONS OF THE XVIIITH CENTURY.

To face p. 110.

nd this numerous company was constantly
newed.

The mother and wife of M. de Montesquiou
ere extremely kind to me. His daughter-in-law,
ho later became governess to Napoleon's son,
as gentle, natural, and very lovable. I had
ten seen him in Paris, and he always seemed to
e very witty, though dry and censorious. At
aupertuis he was gentle and affable—in a word,
together another man. Whenever we happened
be just a few, he would read to us in the evening
i an excellent way. It was at Maupertuis, while
was with child and unwell, that I painted his
ortrait and have never been satisfied with it since.
I remember one evening when we were few
number, the Marquis drew the horoscope of
ich one of us. He foretold I should live a long
hile and become a lovable old woman, because
was not coquettish. Now that I have lived a
ng while, am I a lovable old woman? I doubt
But at least I am an old lover, for I love you
nderly.

CHAPTER X

I DINED SEVERAL TIMES at Saint Oue
with the Duke de Nivernais, who assemble
in a beautiful house the most agreeable socie
in existence.

The Duke de Nivernais, whose grace and refin
ment have become household words, had nob
and gentle manners without the least affectatio
He was noted above all for his extremely galla
behaviour towards women of all ages. In th
respect I might have referred to him as a matchle
example, had I not known Count de Vaudreu
who, though much younger than M. de Niverna
coupled an exquisite gallantry with a politen
that was all the more flattering because it car
from the heart. It is, however, very difficult
convey an adequate idea of the urbanity, t
gracious ease and pleasant manners, which ga
so much charm to Paris society forty ye
ago. The gallantry of which I talk, for instan
has completely vanished. In those days, wom
reigned ; the Revolution dethroned them.

112

The Duke de Nivernais was small and very
[in. Though already very old, when I knew
[m, he was yet full of life. He was passionately
)nd of poetry and wrote charming verses.
I also dined often with the Maréchal de Noailles
: his beautiful château situated at the entrance
) Saint Germain. It had then a very large, well-
ept park. The Maréchal was very nice. His
it and mirth kept all the guests lively. The
.tter he chose from among the literary celebrities
ıd the foremost people of the town and Court.
[is wit was original and effective. He could
ırely resist the desire to express a mischievous
ıought. It was he who said to Louis XV, when
ıe latter discovered the olives he was eating at
ıe hunt were bad : "It must be the bottom
f the barrel, Sire." This remark brings to my
ıind a woman whom I have not yet mentioned,
ıough I knew a good deal about her. She was
woman who sprang from the lowest class of
)ciety and passed through the palace of a king
ı her way to the scaffold, and whose sad end
:ones for the scandalous dazzle of her life. It
as in 1786 that I first went to Louveciennes,
here I had promised to paint Mme Du Barry.
was extremely curious to see this favourite, of
hom I had heard so often. Mme Du Barry
ıust have been then about forty-five years old.
he was big, though not too much so. She was
ıump. Her throat was rather strong but very
:autiful. Her face was still charming, the features
:ing regular and graceful. Her hair was ash-

H   113

coloured and curly like a child's. Only he complexion began to spoil.

She received me very gracefully and seeme to me to have a very good style. I though however, that she was more natural in he mind than in her manners. Besides havin the look of a coquette, for her eyes wer never completely open, she had a pronunciatio that sounded childish and was ill-suited to he age.

She put me up in a suite of rooms behind th machine at Marly which annoyed me terribl with its noise. Underneath my apartment wa a neglected gallery in which was a great disarra of busts, vases, columns, rare marbles and lots o valuable objects. One might have thought the belonged to the mistress of several sovereigns wh had enriched her with their gifts. These relic of grandeur were in direct contrast with th simplicity of the mistress of the house in he clothes and mode of life.

Summer and winter, Mme Du Barry never wor anything but dressing-gown robes of cambric o white muslin, while every day in all weather she went for walks in her park or outside withou any mischievous result, her life in the countr having made her health so robust. She had kep up no relations with the Court that had surrounde her so long. Mme de Souza, the wife of th Portuguese Ambassador, and the Marquise d Brunoy were, I believe, the only women she sav at that time, and during my three visits to he

MADAME LE BRUN.
By herself.

To face p. 115.

ouse, at three different periods, I realized that visitors never troubled her solitude.[1]

I do not know, however, why the Ambassadors of Tippoo-Sahib thought themselves obliged to pay a visit to the former mistress of Louis XV. Not only did they come to Louveciennes, but they brought presents for Mme Du Barry, among other things several pieces of muslin richly embroidered in gold. She gave me one of them, a superb piece of work with large, separate flowers, the colours and gold of which were shaded perfectly.

Most evenings Mme Du Barry and I sat alone by the fireside. Sometimes she talked to me of Louis XV and his Court, always with the greatest respect for the one and the greatest regard for the other. But she avoided all details. It was obvious she preferred to say as little as possible about the matter, so that her conversation was generally rather trifling. Nevertheless, she was a kind woman both in speech and action, and did much good at Louveciennes, where the poor were looked after by her. We often went together to visit some unfortunate man or woman, and I remember her just indignation one day when she saw a woman in child-birth who lacked everything. "How is this!" cried Mme Du Barry. "You have neither linen, nor wine, nor bouillon?"—"Alas! I have nothing, Madam." We went back to the château immediately and Mme Du

[1] I often met there M. de Monville. He was pleasant and very elegant, and took us to see his estate called Le Desert, the house of which was only a layer.

Barry sent for her housekeeper and other servan
who had failed to carry out her orders. I ca
hardly describe her fury against them all, whi
she made them do up a parcel of linen and sei
them off with it at once, together with som
bouillon and Bordeaux wine.

Every day after dinner we took coffee in th
pavilion that is so famous for its style and th
wealth of its adornments. The first time Mn
Du Barry showed it to me she said to me : "
is in this room that Louis XV gave me the honoi
of dining with me. There was a tribune abov
for the musicians who sang during the meal
The salon was delightful. Besides having one
the most beautiful outlooks in the world, it ha
chimneys and doors of most valuable workmanshi
Even the locks could be admired as masterpiec
of the goldsmith's art, while the furniture was
an indescribable richness and elegance.

Louis XV no longer stretched himself out c
those magnificent sofas. His place was taken b
the Duke de Brissac, whom we often left ther
as he liked to take his nap. The Duke de Briss
lived as though settled at Louveciennes, but the
was nothing in his manners or in those of Mn
Du Barry to suggest that he was anything mo
than the friend of the mistress of the châtea
However, it was easy to see that a tender attacl
ment united them. Perhaps it was this vei
attachment that cost them their lives. When Mn
Du Barry crossed over to England before tl
outbreak of the Terror in order to recover h

116

THE COMTESSE DU BARRY.

From the painting by Madame Le Brun (1789).

To facep 117.

tolen diamonds, she was very well received by he English. They did all in their power to prevent her from returning to France. In fact, he was just on the point of leaving when some friends unharnessed her horses. Only her desire to rejoin the Duke de Brissac, whom she had left hidden in her château at Louveciennes, caused her to resist the entreaties of those who wished to keep her in London, where the sale of her diamonds would have maintained her in comfort. To her misfortune, she left and went to rejoin the Duke at Louveciennes. Shortly after, he was arrested before her eyes and thrown into prison at Orleans. From there he was taken with three others, ostensibly for transference to Versailles. All four were put into a tumbril and, scarcely half-way on he journey, ruthlessly massacred !

The bloody head of the Duke de Brissac was taken to Mme Du Barry, and you can imagine how much that unhappy woman must have suffered at the horrible sight. She was not long in succumbing to the fate reserved for those who possessed any fortune, as well as for those who had a great name. She was betrayed and denounced by a little negro called Zamore, who is often mentioned in memoirs of the time as having been overwhelmed with her kindnesses as well as those of Louis XV. Arrested and thrown into prison, Mme Du Barry was judged and condemned to death by the Revolutionary Tribunal at the end of 1793. She was the only woman among so many who perished in those frightful days who was unable to bear the sight of the scaffold She cried out, implored the mercy of the atrociou crowd that surrounded her, and that crowd wa moved to such an extent that the executione made haste to finish his job. This has alway convinced me that if the victims of that execrabl time had not had the noble pride to die courageously the Terror would have ended much sooner. Mer of undeveloped intelligence have too little imagina tion to be moved by an inward suffering, and th people's pity is much more easily excited than it admiration.

I painted three portraits of Mme Du Barry In the first I painted her *en buste*, a small three quarters, attired in a dressing-gown with a stra hat. In the second she is dressed in white satin holding a garland in one hand, while one of he arms leans on a pedestal. I painted this portrai with the utmost care. Like the first, it wa designed for the Duke de Brissac. I saw it agai quite recently. The old General who now own it must have had the head touched up, for it i not the one I painted. It has rouge right up to the eyes, whereas Mme Du Barry never use any. I disown, therefore, this head, which is no my work. The rest of the picture is intact an well preserved. It has just been sold, the Genera having died.

The third portrait of Mme Du Barry by m is in my possession. I began it towards the middl of September 1789. At Louveciennes we hear the sound of endless cannonades, and I remembe

118

the poor woman saying to me : " If Louis XV had been alive, nothing like this would have happened."

I had only painted the head and sketched the figure and arms when I was obliged to make a journey to Paris, hoping to return to finish the portrait. Berthier and Foulon, however, had just been assassinated. My terror was so great that I could think of nothing but leaving the country at once. I left the picture half-finished. I do not know how Count Louis de Narbonne happened to come by it during my absence. On my return to France I received it back from him, and I have now finished it.

The sad contents of this letter warns me that I have come to the period of my life which I should like to be able to forget. I would stifle all memory of it, as I often do, had I not promised to give you a sincere and complete account of my life.

There will no longer be any question of enjoyments, Grecian suppers, or comedies, but days of anguish and terror. I will put off telling you about them till my next letter.

CHAPTER XI

I CANNOT THINK of the last country seats I visited, without finding the memory of my sweetest moments mingled with many a painful memory as well. In 1788, for instance, I went with Robert to stay a few days at Romain-ville, the home of the Maréchal de Ségur. On our way we noticed that the peasants no longer doffed their hats to us. On the contrary, they looked at us insolently, while some even threatened us with their sticks. On arriving at Romainville we were overtaken by a terrible thunderstorm. The sky was of a yellowish colour, tinged with dark grey, and when these terrifying clouds split up, thousands of lightning flashes came out to the accompaniment of fearful thunder and such enormous hailstones that they laid waste the whole of the country forty leagues around Paris. During the storm, Mme de Ségur and I looked at each other with fear and trembling. We seemed to see in that terrible day an omen of the misfortunes which, without being an astrologer, one could have then foretold.

120

That evening and the following day we all went with the Maréchal to look at the sad effect of the storm. Corn, vines, fruit trees—everything was destroyed. The peasants were weeping and tearing at their hair. Everyone hastened to help these unfortunate people. The great landowners gave a lot of money. One rich man immediately distributed forty thousand francs out of his own pocket among the ill-fated people around him. To the shame of mankind, this very man was one of the first to be massacred by the revolutionary cannibals the following year.

The summer of the same year, 1788, I spent a fortnight at Malmaison, which then belonged to the Countess du Molay. Mme du Molay was a very fashionable, pretty woman. Her wit was not electrifying, but she had an intelligent understanding of other people's. Count Olivarés was established in her house at the time, and she had paid him a compliment by having placed at the entrance to a road at the top of the park an inscription bearing the words : " Sierra Morena." Olivarés was not what may be called a pleasant man. The most outstanding feature I noticed about him was his dirtiness. He filled his pockets with Spanish snuff, using them in place of snuff-boxes.

The Duke de Crillon and the dear Abbé Delille came to Malmaison very often, and I was very glad to meet them there. Mme du Molay was very fond of going for lonely walks, while I had a similar preference. So it was agreed that we should carry a sprig of foliage if either of us did not wish to be accompanied or approached. I never went without my sprig, but I threw it away pretty sharp whenever I caught sight of the Abbé Delille.

In June 1789 I went to dine at Malmaison. I found there the Abbé Sieyès and several other friends of the Revolution. M. du Molay raved at the top of his voice against the nobles. Everybody shouted, laying down the law as to all the things necessary for a general upheaval. One could have called it a real club. The conversations frightened me terribly. After dinner the Abbé Sieyés said to one of the persons whose name I've forgotten : " Really, I believe we shall go too far."—" They will go so far that they will get lost on the way," I remarked to Mme du Molay, who had also heard the Abbé and was grieved at so many gloomy portents.

Round about the same time I stayed a few days at Marly with Mme Auguier, the sister of Mme Campan, who was also in the service of the Queen. She had a fine château and park near the machine. One day, as we were together looking out of a window overlooking the courtyard which faced the main road, we saw a drunken man enter and roll on the ground. With her usual kindness, Mme Auguier called her husband's manservant and told him to go and help the poor man, take him to the kitchen and look after him. A few moments later the manservant returned. " You are far too kind, Madame," he said. " The

GRÉTRY.

From the painting by Madame Le Brun (1786).

man is a wretch. Here are the papers that fell out of his pocket." He handed us several copy-books, one of which began thus : " Down with the Royal Family ! Down with the nobles ! Down with the priests ! " Then followed a revolutionary litany and a lot of dreadful predictions, written in a way that made one's hair stand on end. Mme Auguier sent for the Horse Patrol, who were then policing the villages. Four of these military arrived and were requested to take the man away and get information about him. They took him away. The manservant, however, who followed them unobserved, saw them at the turn of the road link arm-in-arm with the prisoner, jumping and singing with him as though they were on the best of terms. I am at a loss to describe how greatly we were frightened by this. What were we coming to, my God ! when the public authority made common cause with the guilty ?

I had advised Mme Auguier to show the copy-books to the Queen. A few days later, being in attendance, she gave them to the Queen to read. Her Majesty returned them, saying : " These things are impossible. I will never believe they are planning such atrocities." Alas ! events were only too soon in removing that noble doubt. And besides the Royal victim who refused to believe such horrors possible, poor Mme Auguier herself was destined to pay for her devotion with her life.

Her devotion never flinched. Knowing that the Queen was without money during the cruel days of the Revolution, she quickly lent her twenty-five louis. The revolutionaries got to know about it and came at once to the palace of the Tuileries to take her to prison, or, rather to the guillotine.

Seeing them arrive with their furious looks and threatening speech, Mme Auguier preferred a prompt death to the anguish of falling into their hands. She threw herself out of the window and was killed.

I have known few women so beautiful and lovable as Mme Auguier. She was tall and shapely. Her face was remarkably fresh-complexioned, milk and rose, and her eyes revealed her loving-kindness. She left two children, whom I have known since their childhood at Marly. One married the Maréchal Ney, the other M. de Broc. The latter girl came to an ill-starred end while yet young. When travelling with Mme Louis Bonaparte, her bosom friend, she went for an excursion to Ancenis and wanted to cross a deep chasm on a plank. The plank gave way beneath her feet and the unfortunate woman plunged to her death in the abyss.

Mme Auguier had two sisters. One was Mme Campan, well known as the first lady-in-waiting to the Queen and as the clever directress of the educational establishment at Saint Germain, where the daughters of all the notabilities of the Empire were educated. I knew Mme Campan at Versailles at the time she enjoyed all the favour and confidence of the Queen. I had no suspicion

AN AMATEUR'S STUDIO IN THE XVIIITH CENTURY

After Dugourc (Musée du Louvre).

To face p. 124.

whatever of her ever failing to keep her devotion and gratitude to her august mistress for so many kindnesses received. When I was staying in St. Petersburg, I heard her accused of having forsaken and betrayed the Queen. Unable to discover anything but the most infamous calumny in such an accusation, I took up the cudgels of defence on behalf of my countrywoman and exclaimed several times: " It is impossible ! " Two years later, on my return to France, I received the following letter from Mme Campan. I copy it so that you may read her justification, which appears to me to bear all the marks of sincerity :

SAINT GERMAIN,
January 27th (Old Style).

At a great distance from me you said, dear Madame : " It is impossible ! " A true mind, goodness and sensibility were the guides of your opinion. These rare qualities, rare indeed in these days, are, happily for me, to be found united in you to talents still more rare. You understand what is impossible for me, as deeply as I am grateful to you for having declared it. In truth, how can one believe I could ever separate for a moment my sentiments, opinions and devotion from everything that I owed to the unfortunate being who, day by day, gave happiness to me and mine, and whose retention of the rights attacked by a perfidious and bloody faction assured happiness for all and especially for me ? I have, on the contrary, had the privilege of giving her undoubted proofs of a gratitude such as she had the right to expect. My poor Sister Auguier and I, though I was not on duty, faced death in order not to leave her during that horrible night of August 10th. After that massacre we remained hidden and frightened to death in the houses of Paris, where we regained strength enough to get as far as the Feuillants

125

and to serve her again during her first detention at the Assembly. Pétion alone separated us from her, when we endeavoured to follow her to the Temple. In face of such true and simple facts, in which I am far from deriving any vanity, you may well ask how it is possible for one to be so oddly calumniated. Was it not because I had to be made to pay dearly for the constant and signal favour shown me during so many years? Is favour at a Court ever forgiven, even when it is bestowed on a person of the household? They tried to disgrace me in the eyes of the Queen, that is all. They did not succeed, however; and one day it will be known to what degree she continued to esteem and trust me in the most important matters. I must, however, add, in order not to disguise anything that may have caused my real sentiments to be misconstrued, that I was never able to bring my mind to accept the emigration plan. I considered it to be harmful to the emigrants, and according to my ideas at that time still more harmful to Louis XVI. Living at the Tuileries, I was constantly struck by the thought that there was only a quarter of a league's distance from the palace to the insurgent suburbs, and a hundred leagues from Coblence or the protecting armies. In mind and feeling women are talkative; far too often I expressed my opinion on this subject, which at that time was the hope of everybody. My fears were inspired by a sentiment utterly different from the mad and criminal love of a dreadful revolutionary. Time has justified them only too well and the numberless victims of that project should prevent those fears from being any longer imputed to me as a crime.

However, I am living at present under a different form. I am entirely devoted to it, with the peace of heart that knows no cause for self-reproach. For some time past I have been longing to show you the outlines of my plan of education, to receive your visit and to pay you my honours as a sincere and valuable friend. Choose a day with interesting and unfortunate Mme Rousseau, and it will be like a feast day for me. Accept my affection, esteem, gratitude and all my devoted sentiments for you.

GENET CAMPAN.

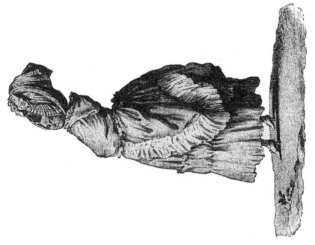

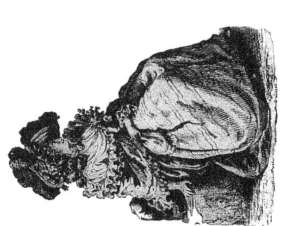

FASHIONS OF THE XVIIIᴛʜ CENTURY.

To face p. 126.

Beside Mme Campan, Mme Auguier had another sister, named Mme Rousseau, a very nice woman, whom the Queen had attached to the service of the first Dauphin. She frequently offered me hospitality, when I had sittings at the Court. The young Prince, whom she attended, became so much attached to her that two days before his death he said to her : " I love you so much, Rousseau, that I shall still love you after death."

Mme Rousseau's husband was fencing-master to the young Princes of France. Hence, being doubly attached to the Royal Family, he was unable to escape death. He was taken and guillotined. I was told that after delivering judgment the judge had the villainy to call out to him : ' Parry that blade, Rousseau ! "

In relating these horrors I am encroaching on the time I have yet to tell you about till the day I left France. In my next letter I will resume the story of the sad events which obliged me to flee from my country in order to find in foreign lands not only my safety but also the kindness which you heaped upon me during my stay in Russia, and of which I keep so sweet a memory.

CHAPTER XII

THE FEARFUL YEAR 1789 had begun and terror had already taken hold of all far-seeing people. I remember how the greater part of the people who came to a concert at my house one evening came in with a distraught look. They had been to the morning parade at Longchamp, when the populace gathered about the Etoile barrier had heaped most dreadful insult on the people who drove past in their carriages. The wretches jumped on to the carriage steps shouting : " Next year it will be your turn to run behind your carriages, while we shall be inside ! " besides a thousand other more infamous remarks. These accounts naturally saddened my evening. I remember noticing that the least alarmed was Mme de Villette, Voltaire's " *belle et bonne.*"

As for me, I had little need to hear fresh detail in order to foresee the dreadful things that were in the making. I knew without a doubt that my house in the Rue du Gros Chenet, where had settled but three months previously, was

128

rked down by the miscreants. Sulphur was own into our cellars through the air-holes. I stood at my window, rude rag-tails would ke their fists at me. Hundreds of sinister ours reached me from all quarters. My life s nothing but a daily round of anxiety and ofound grief.

My health began to weaken visibly. Two good ends of mine, Brongniart the architect and his fe, came to see me and found me so thin and anged that they entreated me to go and stay a w days with them. I gratefully accepted the er. Brongniart had an apartment at the In- lides. I was taken there by a doctor attached the Palais Royal, whose servants wore the leans livery, the only one respected at the he. I was given the best bed. As I was unable eat, I was fed on excellent Bordeaux wine and uillon. Mme Brongniart never left my side. much care should have calmed my spirit, ce my friends saw things in much less sombre ours than I did. Nevertheless, it was impossible them to remove my fear of the evils I foresaw. What's the use of living? What's the use of ing care of oneself?" I often said to my ends, for my fear of the future disgusted me h life. I must say, however, that notwith- nding the depth of my imagination I did not ess but a part of the crimes that were committed er on.

I remember supping at Brongniart's house with de Sombreuil, the Governor of the Invalides

at that time. He told us that an attempt w
going to be made to get hold of the arms he h
in store. " But," he added, " I have hidd
them so thoroughly that I defy them to find them
The good man did not think that it was no long
possible to rely on anybody but oneself. As t
arms were carried off pretty soon after, he w
no doubt betrayed by the servants of the house
had employed.

M. de Sombreuil, whose private virtues were
admirable as his military talents, was among t
prisoners who were to be massacred in the pris
on September 2nd. The assassins spared his l
on account of the tears and supplications of
heroic daughter. Nevertheless, they were atrocic
even in their pardon, for they forced Mlle de Sor
breuil to drink a glass of the blood which was bei
shed in torrents in the prison ! For a very lo
time afterwards the sight of anything red caus
that unhappy girl to vomit distressingly. La
on (in 1794) M. de Sombreuil was sent to t
scaffold by the revolutionary tribunal. These t
events inspired the poet Legouvé with the m
beautiful line of his verses :

Des bourreaux l'ont absous, des juges l'ont frappé,

M. de Sombreuil left a son, who was remarka
for his character and courage. He command
one of the regiments that came from England
Quibéron towards the end of 1795. When
National Convention violated the capitulation sig
by General Hoche, M. de Sombreuil met

MÉNAGEOT.

By Madame Le Brun (Musée de Versailles).

To face p. 131.

death like a brave man. He refused to have his eyes bandaged, and himself gave the order to shoot. At the moment of execution Tallien said to him : " Sir, you come from a very unfortunate family."—" I came to avenge it," replied M. de Sombreuil. " But I am only able to imitate it."

Mme Brongniart took me for a walk behind the Invalides. Near by were some peasants' houses. While we were sitting against one of these hovels we overheard the conversation of two men who were unaware of our presence. " If you want to earn ten francs," said one, " come and help us make a row. You've only got to shout : Down with this ! Down with the other ! And above all shout as loud as ever against Bayonne."—" Ten francs are worth having," answered the other. " But shan't we get cudgelled ? "—" What next ! " rejoined the first. " We are the people who do the cudgelling." You can imagine what effect was produced on me by this dialogue.

The following day we happened to pass in front of the iron railings of the Invalides, where there was an immense crowd of those nasty people who had made a habit of walking up and down under the galleries of the Palais Royal. They were all ragged vagabonds, neither peasants nor workmen, obviously with no occupation but that of bandits, judging from their frightful faces. Mme Brongniart, who kept a stouter heart than I, tried to reassure me. But I was so frightened

that I was about to turn back home, when we
saw a horse arrive with a young woman in the
saddle, wearing a riding habit and a hat with black
plumes. The horrible gang immediately made way
for the young woman, who was followed by tw'
riders in the Orleans livery. I recognized a
once the beautiful Pamela, whom Mme de Genli
had brought to my house. She was then in al
the beauty of her freshness and truly ravishing
We heard the whole horde cry out : " Here yo
are ! Here's the one we ought to have for Queen ! '
Pamela went on riding up and down in the mids
of that disgusting mob, which led me to some very
gloomy reflections.[1]

Shortly after I returned to my house, but wa
unable to go on living there. Society seemed to
me breaking up altogether, honest folk being
without any protection whatever, for the Gard
Nationale was so oddly made up that it revealed
a mixture as weird as it was frightful. Fea
showed its effects on everybody, Pregnant wome
I saw passing made me feel quite sad ; most o
them were jaundiced with fright. In this respec
I have noticed that the generation born durin
the Revolution is much less robust than its fore
runner. How many children must have bee
born weak and ailing in those sad days !

M. de Riviére, the Chargé d'Affaires of Saxony
whose daughter married my brother, came t
offer me his hospitality. I spent two weeks a

---

[1] She afterwards married Lord Fitzgerald. She is his widow now, bein
still alive though much altered.

THE HÔTEL DE BEAUVAU IN THE FAUBOURG SAINT-HONORÉ.

After Lallemand.

To face p. 133.

least in his house. It was there that I saw the busts of the Duke of Orleans and M. Necker carried in procession, followed by a great crowd shouting that one would be their king and the other their protector. The same evening these honest folk came back. They set fire to the barrier at the end of our street (Rue Chaussée d'Antin), tore up the paving and erected barricades, shouting : " The enemy is coming ! " The enemy never came : alas ! the enemy was in Paris.

Though I was treated at M. de Riviére's like one of his children, and was able to feel safe under his roof, as he was a Foreign Minister, I had made up my mind to leave France. For several years I had been longing to go to Rome. The great number of portraits I had undertaken to paint was the sole cause of my delay. However, if the moment for departure was ever to arrive, it had certainly come at that time. I could no longer paint. My imagination was darkened and wilted by so many horrors, and ceased to find satisfaction in my art. Moreover, frightful libels were being poured out on my friends and acquaintances, even on myself, alas ! Though I had never harmed anyone, my thoughts were very much like those of the man who said : " They accuse me of having taken the towers of Notre-Dame. They are still in their place ; but I am going off, for it is obvious they have a grudge against me."

I left several portraits I had begun, including

that of Mme Contat. I refused also to paint Mlle de la Borde (later Duchess de Noailles), who was brought to me by her father. She was hardly sixteen years old and charming. But for me there was no longer any question of success and fortune. The only question was how to save one's head. Consequently, I had my carriage loaded and had got my passport ready to leave with my daughter and governess on the following day, when I saw my drawing-room invaded by a great crowd of National Guards with firearms. Most of them were drunk, ill-dressed and horrible looking. Some of them came up to me and told me in the rudest language that I was not to leave and would have to remain. I answered that everybody was now called to enjoy freedom and that I wished to avail myself of it on my own account. They scarcely listened to me, and kept repeating : " You shall not leave, citizeness, you shall not leave." At last they went away. I was still writhing with anxiety when I saw two others enter. They did not frighten me, however, though they were of the same band, for I was quick to comprehend that they did not wish me any harm. " Madame," said one, " we are your neighbours. We have come to advise you to leave as soon as possible. You could not go on living here. You are so altered that we feel sorry for you. But don't go in your carriage. Take the diligence. It is safer."

I thanked them with all my heart, and followed their good advice. I sent out to have three places

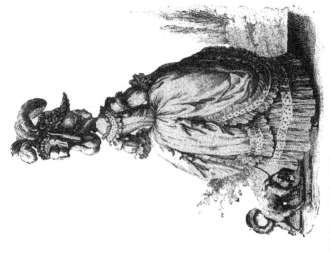

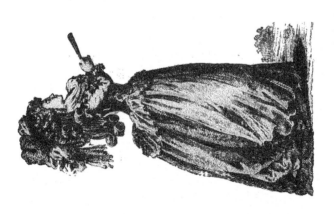

FASHIONS OF THE XVIIItʜ CENTURY.

reserved, wishing to take with me my daughter, who was then about five or six years old. I was unable to get the places till a fortnight later, since all the people who were emigrating were leaving, like me, by diligence.

At last the long-awaited day arrived. It was the 5th of October, the same day the King and Queen were brought from Versailles to Paris in the midst of pikes! My brother witnessed the arrival of their Majesties at the Hôtel de Ville. He heard the speech of M. Bailly, and knowing that I was to leave during the night, he came to my house about ten o'clock in the evening. " Never," he told me, " was the Queen more like a Queen than she was to-day, when she came looking so calm and noble in the midst of those madmen." Then he told me of the beautiful answer she had given M. Bailly: " I have seen everything, known everything, and I have forgotten everything."

The events of that journey overwhelmed me with so great an anxiety for the welfare of their Majesties, and of all people of standing, that at midnight I was dragged out to the diligence in an indescribable state. I was very much afraid of the Faubourg St. Antoine, which I had to traverse in order to reach the Trône turnpike-gate. My brother, M. Robert and my husband accompanied me as far as that gate, without leaving the coach door for one moment. The Faubourg, which we feared so much, was perfectly peaceful. All the inhabitants, workers and others,

had been to Versailles to fetch the Royal Family
and the fatigue of the journey kept them all asleep

The man sitting opposite me in the diligence
was extremely dirty and stank like the pest. He
calmly related to me how he had stolen some
watches and other property. Happily he saw
nothing on me to tempt him. I was taking very
little linen with me and only eighty louis for the
journey. I had left my belongings and jewels in
Paris, while the fruit of my labours remained
in the hands of my husband, who spent every
thing, as I have already related.[1]

The thief was not satisfied with telling us about
his high deeds. He incessantly talked of hanging
people from lamp-posts, naming a host of persons
of my acquaintance. My daughter thought the
man very wicked. He frightened her so much
that I took courage from the occasion to say to
him : "I beg you, Sir, not to speak of murder
before this child." He held his tongue and ended
up by playing a game of bataille with my daughter

On the same seat with me was a violent Jacobin
from Grenoble. He was about fifty years old
ugly and bilious-looking. Every time we stopped
at an inn for dinner or supper he started spouting
his ideas in the most terrifying fashion. At all
the towns a crowd of people stopped the diligence
in order to hear the news from Paris. Our
Jacobin would then cry out : "Be at rest, my

[1] I maintained myself abroad by painting portraits. Far from sending
me any money, M. Le Brun wrote me such pitiful letters about his distress
that I sent him a thousand écus on one occasion and a hundred louis on
another. I also sent the same sum to my mother later on.

children. We've got the baker and his wife in Paris. We'll make a Constitution for them. They'll be obliged to accept it, and that will be the end of the story." The simpletons, whose heads were being turned in this fashion, believed the man like an oracle. All this made my journey very sad. I no longer had any fear for myself; I was anxious about my mother, brother, friends, everybody. I shuddered at the thought of their Majesties' fate, for all along the route, almost as far as Lyons, horsemen kept coming up to the diligence to tell us that the King and Queen had been massacred and Paris set on fire. My poor little daughter was trembling all over, thinking she saw her father and our house being burnt. I no sooner succeeded in quietening her than another horseman would dash up and repeat the same horrible story.

At last I arrived at Lyons. I drove to the house of M. Artaut, a merchant, whom I had sometimes received at my house in Paris together with his wife. I knew neither of them but slightly. They had inspired me with confidence, since we shared the same opinions concerning all that was happening. My first care was to ask them whether it was true that the King and Queen had been massacred. Thank Heaven, I was reassured for that once.

M. and Mme Artaut had some difficulty in recognizing me at first, not only because I had altered to such an extent, but also because I was wearing the costume of a badly dressed workwoman with a large kerchief falling over my eyes. I had had occasion during my journey to congratulate myself for having taken this precaution. I had just exhibited at the Salon a portrait of myself with my daughter in my arms. The Jacobin from Grenoble spoke about the exhibition and even praised the portrait. I shuddered lest he should recognize me. I used all my cunning to hide my face from him. Thanks to that and my costume, I came through with nothing worse than a little fear.

I spent three days at Lyons with the Artaut family. I greatly needed the rest. Apart from my hosts, I saw no one in the town, being anxious to keep the strictest incognito. M. Artaut engaged a coachman for me, telling him I was a relation of his. He strongly commended me to this good man, who indeed showed every possible care to me and my daughter.

I am at a loss to tell you what I felt as I crossed the bridge at Beauvoisin. There at last, I began to breathe. I was outside of France, that France which was my country notwithstanding, and which I blamed myself for leaving with joy. The sight of the mountains, however, distracted me from all my thoughts. I had never seen high mountains before. Those of Savoy seemed to me to touch the sky, mingling with them in a dense mist. My first feeling was one of fear, but I insensibly grew accustomed to the sight and ended by admiring them.

The landscape about the road of the Echelles

138

CALONNE, MINISTER OF STATE, CONTROLLER-GENERAL
OF FINANCE.

By Madame Le Brun.

To face p 138.

enchanted me. I fancied I was looking at the Gallery of the Titans. I have always called it thus ever since. Wishing to enjoy all these beautiful scenes more thoroughly, I got out of the carriage. About half-way along the road, however, I was seized with a great terror. A part of the rocks was being worked with gun-powder, and the effect of this was like thousands of cannon-shots. Echoing from rock to rock, the noise was infernal.

I went up Mount Cenis at the same time as several strangers. A postilion came up to me and said : " Madame should take a mule, as it is too fatiguing for a lady like you to go on foot." I replied that I was a workwoman quite accustomed to walking. " Ah ! " he laughingly rejoined, " Madame is no workwoman. It is known who you are."—" Well, who am I ? " I asked.—" You are Madame Le Brun, who paints so perfectly. We are all very glad to know you are far away from the evil-doers." I have never been able to make out how this man knew my name. It proved to me, however, what a lot of emissaries the Jacobins must have had. Happily I was no longer in fear of them. I was beyond their loathsome power. Instead of my native country, I was going to dwell in places where the arts flourished and civilized manners prevailed. I was going to visit Rome, Naples, Berlin, Vienna, Petersburg, and above all, though I did not know at the time, I was going to find you, dear friend, know you, and love you.

THE ABBÉ DELILLE.

JAQUES DELILLE was nothing but a child all his life, the most lovable, best and wittiest child imaginable. He was nicknamed Chose Légère, which has always struck me as being most appropriate. No man, indeed, ever skimmed life so lightly as he, making no strong attachment to anything whatever in the world. Enjoying the present without thinking of what was to follow, he rarely troubled his mind with a deep thought. It was extremely easy for anyone desirous of gaining a hold over him to win his affections and lead him. His marriage is sufficient proof of that. How often he complained of the yoke he was wearing when there was still time to cast it off! At last a friend persuaded him to take his freedom and offered him a shelter. Delille accepted the offer. Delighted and full of resolve, he only asked for an hour in which to go and get some belongings. Evening came and the friend waited in vain for Delille to appear. So he went to find him. " Well ? " he said.—" Well," replied Delille, " I am going to marry her, my friend. I hope you will consent to act as witness."

Count de Choiseul-Gouffier, an intimate friend of his, who was about to leave for Greece, had

MADAME DE BRUNOY'S HOUSE IN THE CHAMPS-ELYSÉES.

After Lallemand.

To face p. 140.

often spoken to him of his desire to take him as a companion on the journey. Nothing, however, was agreed upon. On the day of his departure the Count went to the Abbé and said to him : " I am leaving this instant. Come with me. The carriage is ready." And the Abbé got into the carriage without making the least preparation, though M. de Choiseul had, in fact, provided for that.

Arrived at Marseilles, Delille went for a walk along the shore and gazed at the sea. A deep melancholy came over him. He said : " I shall never be able to put that immensity between my friends and me. No, I will not go any farther." So he slipped secretly away from M. de Choiseul and hid himself in a little tavern, where he thought himself safe from discovery. After much searching, however, he was tracked down by M. de Choiseul, who took him on board with him.

Though far from his friends, he never forgot them and often sent them news of himself. He wrote to me from Athens several times. In one of his letters he told me he had written my name on the Temple of Minerva. I remembered this when I was at Naples, and wrote to him that with much more reason I had written his name on the tomb of Virgil. I shall always regret having lost the Abbé's letters, as well as those which I received from M. de Vaudreuil during his travels in Spain with Count d'Artois, which were full of interesting details on that country. I entrusted them to my brother when I left France, and when the searching of houses became the order of the day, he judged it prudent to burn the correspondence.

The Abbé Delille spent his life in high society, where he was a very brilliant ornament. Not only did he recite his verses in a delightful manner, but his fine wit and natural mirth rendered his conversation most charming. He was matchless as a story-teller, delighting every group with scores of tales and anecdotes with never a drop of gall or satire. Hence it may be said that everybody liked him, just as he may be said to have liked everybody. The latter merit, if indeed it is one, was due, I think, to that weakness of his character which I have already referred to. He knew no more how to hate than to resist, and in the ordinary things of life his easy-going manner was truly rare. For instance, he may have promised to dine with you. At the moment of setting out for your house, if another person came to get him he would go off with him, leaving you to wait in vain. I remember one day reproaching him with having failed to keep his promise in this way. He proved to us that he had a ready answer for everything. " I take it," he said, " that the person who comes to fetch me is much more urgent than the person who waits."

He had traits of good-nature that reminded one very much of La Fontaine. One evening, when he came to supper at my house, I said to him : " M. l'Abbé, it is very late. You live so far away that I feel uneasy at seeing you go home at this hour, driving your cabriolet."—He answered : " I always

142

Son génie et son cœur se peignent dans ses yeux ;
Le plaisir est chez lui compagnon de la gloire ;
Disciple de Virgile et son rival heureux,
Il vole sur ses pas au Temple de Mémoire.

De S.

THE ABBÉ DELILLE.

After Miger.

To face p 142.

take the precaution of carrying a night-cap in my pocket." I suggested making a bed for him in my salon. "No, no!" he said. "I have a friend in your street where I often go for a lodging. It doesn't put him out in the least, and I can go there at any time." Which he did at once.

No one enjoyed life or skimmed its charm as much as he. Always ready to laugh and be amused, he had a sort of happiness like that of a child. The same man, however, displayed the utmost energy during the whole time of the Revolution. Everybody knows how courageously he rebuffed Chaumette, the Attorney of the Commune, who commanded him in 1793 to write an ode to the Goddess of Reason. Delille was quite aware that his refusal meant sentence of death, and it was then he wrote his beautiful verses on the immortality of the soul. He read them to Chaumette till he came to the following lines :

> Oui, vous qui, de l'Olympe usurpant le tonnerre,
> Des éternelles lois renversez les autels ;
> Lâches oppresseurs de la terre,
> Tremblez, vous êtes immortels ! [1]

He stopped, looked at the Tribune, and repeated in a strong, assured voice : "Vous aussi, tremblez vous êtes immortel." Though much taken aback, Chaumette stammered a few threats. "I am quite ready," replied Delille. "I have just read my will." For this once the good man's courage led to a happy result, for Chaumette left him in

[1] "Yes, you, who usurp the thunders of Olympus and overturn the altars of the eternal laws, base oppressors of earth, tremble, you are immortal !"

143

order to go and tell his friends that it was not yet time to put Delille to death. After which he never ceased to give Delille his protection. Nevertheless the poet thought it prudent to go abroad. He crossed to England, where he was received and made much of by all the notabilities.

His Muse always kept his fire sacred to his lawful sovereigns. During the reign of the world-shaking usurper, he published his poem " La Pitié," and on his return to France, had the courage, perhaps still more rare, to resist the false caresses of an absolute power. He did not fear to lay himself open to disgrace in order to preserve his own esteem, the esteem of his friends and the general admiration, which he enjoyed till the day of his death.

Count de Vaudreuil.

Born to high rank, Count de Vaudreuil owed much more to Nature than to his position, though the latter overwhelmed him with all its gifts. To the advantages of a high position in the world, he united all the qualities that make a man agreeable. He was big, well-made and carried himself with remarkable elegance and nobility. His look was gentle and fine, his features extremely mobile like his ideas, while his smile was pre-possessing from the start. He had plenty of wit, but one was tempted to believe that he did not open his mouth except to get the best out of yours, for he listened to you in so friendly and courteous a manner. Whether the conversation

is serious or joking, he knew how to adopt any
ne, any nuance, for he was as well-informed as
was gay. He was an excellent story-teller,
d I know verses by him which might be quoted
th honour by the most hard to please. These
rses, however, were never read except by his
ends. He was all the less anxious to have
em published because he employed in several
e spirit and form of the epigram. In order to
this, his pure and noble soul must have been
rred to revolt by a bad deed, and one may
ily say that if he showed small pity for what
s evil, he gloried mightily in all that was good.
ibody outdid him in warmth of service to
ise who enjoyed his esteem. If his friends were
acked, he defended them with so much energy
it cold folk accused him of exaggeration. "You
ist judge me in that way," he said to an egotist
our acquaintance, "for I respond to everything
id, while you respond to nothing."
The society he preferred was that of artists and
foremost men of letters. He had many friends
ong them, whom he always kept, even though
ir political opinions were not the same as his.
He was passionately fond of all the arts, while
knowledge of painting was remarkable. As
fortune allowed him to satisfy very expensive
es, he collected a gallery of masterpieces of
ous schools. His salon was adorned with
table furniture and ornaments of excellent
e. He frequently gave magnificent parties,
were so fairylike that he was called the

magician. His greatest joy, however, was to bri
relief to the unfortunate. Hence the great num
of thankless people he made !

The only contradiction to be found in t
wholesome and upright spirit was that M.
Vaudreuil very often complained of living at
Court, whereas it was obvious to all his frie1
that he would not have been able to live elsewhe
Nevertheless I think I can explain the cause
this oddness. The fine quality of his soul m;
him a child of Nature, which he loved and co1
enjoy but too rarely. His rank kept him ;
often away from the society to which he gravita
by reason of his solid understanding and affect
for the arts. On the other hand, he was
doubt pleased to occupy so distinguished a posit
at the Court, which he owed to the personal m
of his sincere and loyal character. Moreover,
adored his Prince, the Count d'Artois, whom
never flattered and never forsook in his n
fortune. Such a friendship rarely grows
between two men, when one is born near
the Throne. Their friendship, indeed, was muti
In 1814, M. de Vaudreuil happened to fall i
a dispute with the Count d'Artois, and on ;
account he wrote him a long letter saying r
cruel it seemed to him to disagree after thi
years of friendship. The Prince answered l
in two lines : " Hold your tongue, old fool, ;
have lost your memory, for it is forty years i
I have been your best friend."

During the emigration, at an advanced age,
146

married a young and pretty cousin of his in England. He had two sons and was as good a husband as father. Years of misfortune, including the loss of his fortune, which was not restored to him by the Restoration, never succeeded in crushing him. He kept the same heart and spirit till his last breath.

At the Restoration he was appointed Governor of the Louvre. So it will be noted that he ended his days near the place enclosing the masterpieces he had so much admired during his life. His gentle soul felt the need of lifting its affections above this earth, and accordingly he became very devout, though without any sanctimoniousness. These sentiments assuaged his end, and he died surrounded by his friends, in the arms of his beloved Prince, who never left him. The following verses addressed to M. de Vaudreuil by the poet Lebrun justify what I have said:

A M. Le Comte De Vaudreuil.

Une Grâce, une Muse, en effet, m'a remis
Les jolis vers dictés par le dieu du Parnasse
          Au plus céleste des amis,
A Mécène—Vaudreuil, qui chante comme Horace,
Eh quoi ! l'ennui des courts n'a donc rien qui vous glace ?
Quoi ! votre luth brilliant n'est jamais détendu ?
Vous puisez dans votre âme un art divin de plaire,
Et vous joignez toujours le bien dire au bien faire.
Horace avec plaisir chez vous s'était perdu ;
Vous en avez si bien l'esprit et le langage,
          Que par un charmant badinage
          Vous me l'avez deux fois rendu.

COUNTESS DE SABRAN
(Afterwards Marquise de Boufflers).

I made her acquaintance a few years befo
the Revolution. She was then very good-lookin
her blue eyes expressing her refinement and goo
ness. She was fond of the arts and literatur
wrote very fine verses, and was a wonderful stor
teller. All this without showing the least pr
tentiousness. Her naïve and merry spirit had ;
attractive simplicity which led to her being mu
loved and courted, though she made no attem
to pride herself on her numerous successes :
society. As for the qualities of her heart, it
enough to say that her great affection for h
son did not prevent her from having many frienc
to whom she always remained devoted and faithfu

Mme de Sabran was one of the women I sa
most, visited and received at my house with th
utmost pleasure. In her company one was nev
bored. I was therefore delighted to find her
Prussia during the emigration. She was th
staying at Reinsberg in the house of Prince Henr
as was also the Chevalier de Boufflers, whom s
afterwards married. In the last years of her li
when she returned to France she became blin
Her son never left her side. His arm was, so
speak, attached to that of his mother. His ta
was truly enviable, for in spite of her ailmer
and age, Mme de Boufflers was always good ar
kind and kept the charm that pleases and attra
everybody. I remember how, towards the end
148

THE COMTESSE DE SABRAN.
By Madame Le Brun.

To face p 149.

her life, after being operated on for cataract by Forlense, the famous oculist, she was obliged to live in darkness. When I went to see her one evening, I found her all alone in the dark. I thought I would only stay for a moment, but the ever-reviving charm of her witty conversation, so full of anecdotes related as none but she was able, kept me more than three hours by her side. Listening to her, I thought that, seeing nothing and receiving no stimulus from outside objects, she was reading within herself, if I may say so, and that sort of magic lantern of things and ideas which she described to me with so much beauty held me to the spot. I left her with regret, for I had never found her more lovable.

Mme de Boufflers left two children. Her son, Count de Sabran, is well known not only for his subtle wit but also on account of the charming fables he recites so perfectly. Her daughter, Mme de Custine, was known to me in the days of her youth, when she was like Spring itself. She was passionately fond of painting and copied the great masters to perfection. So well did she imitate their colouring and vigour that, on going into her study one day, I mistook her copy for the original. She did not hide from me the pleasure she derived from my mistake, for she was just as natural as she was nice and beautiful.

THE POET LEBRUN.

I do not believe I admired any living poet so much as Lebrun, who had assumed the name of

Pindare. The lofty character of his poetry filled me with so great an enthusiasm that I conceived a real friendship for the poet. Though his conceit was amazing, I found him so natural that it never crossed my mind for a moment to find anything ridiculous in it. Thus, when Lebrun finished the ode entitled *Exegi Monumentum*, he read it out to us. It included the following verses :

> Comme un cèdre aux vastes ombrages
> Mon nom, croissant avec les âges,
> Regne sur la posterité.
> Siècles, vous êtes ma conquête ;
> Et la palme, qui ceint ma tête
> Rayonne d'immortalité.[1]

Nobody, however, found anything to say about it except : " Wonderful ! How true ! "

Lebrun frequently came to my house. I never arranged a little gathering without inviting him among the first. My admiration for his talent made me so fond of him that I could not suffer to hear any evil about him. Once I was entertaining some people to dinner, when I heard his morals being attacked in the gravest fashion.

Among other things, it was said that he had sold his wife to the Prince de Conti. Naturally I refused to believe a word of the story. I was furious. " Haven't I also been slandered ? " I said in my anger. " Look at all the absurd things that are said about me concerning M. de Calonne. What you say is not a bit more true, I am sure."

[1] " Like a cedar with a vast shade, my name, growing with the ages, reign over posterity. Ages, I am your conqueror ; and the palm that wreathe my brow, beams with immortality."

PONCE-ECHOUARD, THE POET.

After Beauminil.

To face p. 151.

However, finding I was unable to convince his accusers, I got up and left the table to shed tears in my bedroom. Doyen arrived and found me weeping. "Ho! what is the matter, my child?" he asked.—"I couldn't put up with those men," I replied. "They are calumniating Lebrun in a horrible way." I told him what had been said. He smiled. "I don't assume that it is all true," he said. "But you are too young, my dear friend, to realize that most geniuses have everything at their country house and nothing at their town house; in other words, everything in the head and nothing in the heart."

Later on I often recalled this saying of Doyen's. When I made Lebrun's acquaintance, he was very poor and always miserably dressed. M. de Vaudreuil was not long in appreciating his fine talent, and secretly sent him a large coffer filled with clothes and linen. I do not know whether the poet discovered the author of this anonymous gift. But it is a fact that when the Revolution came he did not vociferate against M. de Vaudreuil as much as he did against many others. It is true that M. de Vaudreuil neglected no occasion to make him known and to spread his reputation. Lebrun had not yet had anything printed when the Count was delighted with the ode on Courtisans and spoke about it to the Queen, who expressed a desire to hear it. M. de Vaudreuil made haste to get the ode and read it to Her Majesty. When he had finished, the Queen said to him: "Do you know that he is taking away our wrapping?"

M. de Vaudreuil told me of this true remark
It struck me much more than it struck him, fo:
he refused to see in the poem anything bu
poetized philosophy, whereas Lebrun and his like
were preaching with a view to the future. The
proof of this is found in the Revolution wher
Pindare became atrocious. His strophes on the
death of the King and Queen are infernal. To
the shame of his memory, I would like to have
them printed opposite the quatrain he composed
on the day the King granted him a pension, and
which ended thus :

> Larmes qui n'avait pu m'arracher le malheur,
> Coulez pour la reconnaissance.[1]

Far from that, however, kind M. Desprès ha
suppressed all the horrors in the new collection
of Lebrun's poems, hoping, no doubt, to confine
them to oblivion for ever. For my part, I prefe
that justice should be done whatever the man'
talent may have been.

When I returned to France, Lebrun was stil
alive. Neither of us, however, had any desire to
see each other again.

CHAMFORT.

Of all the men of letters who came to my house
there was one I always detested, as if by inspiration
of the future. That was Chamfort. I received
him, nevertheless, very often, out of deference
for several of my friends, especially M. de Vaudreuil

[1] " Tears, which misfortune could not draw from me, flow with gratitude.

whose heart he had gained in his misery. His conversation was very witty, though tart, full of gall, and without any charm for me. Moreover, I greatly disliked his synicism and dirtiness. His real name was Nicolas. He changed it, however, on the advice of M. de Vaudreuil, who wished to push him forward in the world and, if possible, even at Court. M. de Vaudreuil accommodated him in great style at his house and, being almost always absent at Versailles, had a table served for Chamfort and the people he cared to invite. He treated the man like a brother. Yet this man, on being reproached later on by his friends, the revolutionaries, with having lived in the house of a *former nobleman*, cowardly answered : " What does it matter ? I was Plato at the Court of the tyrant Denys." Now, I ask what sort of tyrant was M. de Vaudreuil ! And what sort of Plato was Chamfort !

His intimate connections with Mirabeau, and, above all, his envy of the great, which had long been gnawing at his heart, were not slow to make Chamfort a demoniacal partisan of the Revolution. Forgetting, or rather recalling, that he had been secretary of the establishments of the Prince de Condé and the Princess Elisabeth, both of whom had overwhelmed him with favours, he revealed himself as one of the most ardent enemies of the throne and nobility. In spite of the proverb that wolves do not devour one another, Chamfort was put into prison by the very people he had served so well with his voice and pen, and after being arrested a second time he cut his throat with a razor.

THE MARQUISE DE GROLLIER.

Mme de Grollier, though not very fond of society, was well known in high life, which she adorned with her superior mind. Her education was far beyond what was usually given to women. She knew Latin and Greek and was thoroughly conversant with the classic masters ; but in a salon she concealed her learning and showed only her wit. A middling person is apt to show off any slight instruction. Mme de Grollier, how- ever, was always simple and natural, manifesting no pretence or pedantry.

In the early days of my marriage, I went about in the world very little, preferring the small gatherings of the Marquise de Grollier to crowded assemblies. I often passed the whole evening with her alone, much to my satisfaction. Her conversation was always lively and full of ideas and sallies. Nevertheless, there was never a word of evil-speaking in all the witty sayings that constantly poured from her lips. This is all the more remarkable because this very superior woman owed her perfect knowledge of the world to her tact and subtle mind, and also because she was somewhat misanthropic. This was often proved to me by the things she said.

For instance, she had a dog which became the joy of her life when she grew blind and deaf. I, too, had a dog of which I was very fond. One

154

MADAME MOLÉ-REYMOND.
By Madame Le Brun.

To face p. 154.

day when we were talking about the devotion and fidelity of our two little animals, I said : "I wish dogs could speak. They would tell us such lovely things ! "—" My dear," she replied, "if they could speak, they would hear, and that would soon spoil them."

Mme de Grollier painted flowers with great superiority. Far from being what is called the talent of an amateur, her talent was such that many of her pictures could be placed beside those of Van Spaendonck, whose pupil she was. She was a wonderful talker on painting, as she was on all subjects, for I never left her salon without having learnt something interesting or instructive. I never left her without regret, and I had grown so accustomed to visiting her that my coachman drove me there without my saying a word to him, which she often pointed out to me in a very pleasant way.

Just as pictures require shades, so several persons have reproached Mme de Grollier with exaggeration in her sentiments and opinions. Certainly, she was rather high-flown in everything. But the result was so much greatness of heart and nobility of soul that she owed to her temperament many true friends, who remained faithful to her till her last day. Moreover, no one had so much charm of manner as Mme de Grollier, or the perfect tone which is unknown nowadays and seems to have died with her. For she is dead, alas ! and that thought is one of the saddest of my life. She died in full possession of the lofty faculties of her mind.

I was told that shortly before she expired she sat up and raising her eyes to heaven, her white hair dishevelled, she breathed a prayer to God that brought tears to the eyes of all who heard her, at the same time filling them with admiration. She prayed for herself, her country, and for the Restoration which she believed should bring happiness to France. She spoke a long while, as did Homer and Bossuet, and then breathed her last.

MADAME DE GENLIS.

I made the acquaintance of Mme de Genlis before the Revolution. She came to see me, presented me to the young Princes of Orleans, whom she was educating, and a little later brought me Pamela, whom I thought as beautiful as it is possible to be. Mme de Genlis was very proud of that young person, and endeavoured to bring out all her charms. I remember she used to make her strike various attitudes, raise her eyes to heaven, give various expressions to her beautiful face. Though all this was very nice to look at, I thought that so deep a study of coquetry might be too much of a good thing for the pupil.

Mme de Genlis' conversation always seemed to me better than her literary works, though some of them are charming, especially *Mademoiselle de Clermont*, which I consider to be her masterpiece. Her conversation, however, had a certain sprightliness and on several points a certain frankness that is absent in her works.

She was a delightful story-teller and had a

MADAME SAINT-HUBERT.

By Le Moine.

To face p 156.

great store of tales; I think nobody at Court or in town had seen so many people and things as she had done. There was a charm in her simplest remarks that can hardly be described. Her expressions were so attractive and her choice of words so tasteful that one felt inclined to write down all she said.

On my return from my travels she came to see me one morning. As she had forewarned me of her visit, I informed several of my acquaintances, some of whom did not like Mme de Genlis at all. She had scarcely started to converse, when friends and foes alike were delighted, and listened, as though enchanted, to her brilliant conversation for more than half an hour.

Mme de Genlis could never have been exactly good-looking. She was tall and well-made, and had well-defined features with a very fine look and smile. I think it would have been difficult for her face to express good-nature; but it assumed every other expression with an amazing mobility.

MADAME DE VERDUN.

Though not a celebrity like the woman I have just spoken of, Mme de Verdun may be remembered for her very fine and natural disposition. Her good nature and mirth made her a general favourite, and I may regard it as one of the joys of my life that she should have been my first, and still remains my best, friend. Her husband was Fermier-Général. He was outwardly a cold man, but full of wit and good nature, and was unable to see unfortunate people without hastening to help them. He owned the Château de Colombes near Paris.

This château was inhabited once upon a time by Queen Henrietta of England. The walls of the salons and galleries were almost all painted by Simon Vouet. The damp, however, had tarnished his remarkable paintings, and M. de Verdun, who was a great art-lover and connoisseur, undertook to renovate them with complete success.

I very often went to stay at the château for several days. M. and Mme de Verdun used to entertain the most agreeable society, composed of artists, men of letters and people of wit. Carmontelle, who was an intimate friend of our hosts, was a great resource. He made us act his proverbs. Moreover, the conversation in general was so lively that we were never overtaken by boredom.

It would be useless nowadays to try to find the delight that came from the charming conversation of those days.

The Abbé Delille wrote to me at Rome: "Politics has ruined everything; no one converses any more in Paris." On my return to France I realized the truth of these words only too well. Go into any salon you like, you will find there the women yawning in a circle and the men up in a corner quarrelling over some law or other. We have seen the last, among a good many other things, of what used to be called conversation; that is to say, one of the greatest charms of French society.

HUBERT ROBERT.

After the painting by Madame Le Brun.

To face p. 158.

The Revolution put an end to all the pleasures of Colombes. As M. de Verdun was known to be very rich, it was not long before he was put into prison. One can imagine the despair of his adoring wife. It must be said for the honour of mankind, that as soon as the news of his arrest reached Colombes the peasants assembled and went to Paris to beg with tears in their eyes for the release of their benefactor.

The result of this action was to prevent the authorities from daring to put him to death. Nevertheless he was still a prisoner, when the good folk came a second time and renewed their request with so much earnest that they secured his release at last. When Mme de Verdun heard the news, she was so overjoyed that she lost her head and sent two carriages to fetch her husband from prison, thinking that two would get there quicker than one.

ROBERT.

Robert, the landscape painter, excelled in painting ruins. His pictures in this genre are fit to be placed next to those of Jean Paul Panini. It was very fashionable and grand to have one's salon painted by Robert. Hence the number of pictures by him is amazing. Certainly, they are far from being all of the same degree of beauty. Robert possessed that happy facility which may be called fatal. He painted a picture as fast as he wrote a letter. But when he controlled his facility, his works were often perfect. Some of his pictures go very well beside those of Vernet.

Of all the artists I knew, Robert went about most in society, where, moreover, he was very much liked.

Fond of all the pleasures, not excepting that of eating, he was much in demand. I do not believe he dined at home more than three times a year. Plays, balls, dinners, concerts, country parties or any other pleasure, were never refused by him, for he spent in amusement all the time he was not working.

He was natural, well-educated and free from pedantry, while the inexhaustible brightness of his disposition made him one of the pleasantest men in society. He was always famous for his skill in physical exercises, and at an advanced age still retained the preferences of his youth. At the age of sixty and more, though very fat, he remained so agile that he ran better than anyone else in a game of hide-and-seek. He played tennis and ball, and made us weep with laughter at the schoolboy tricks he performed to amuse us. For instance, at Colombes he once chalked a long line on the drawing-room floor and dressed like a mountebank, with a balancing pole in his hands, walked solemnly or ran up and down the line, imitating so well the attitudes and gestures of a tight-rope dancer that the illusion was perfect. Nothing so funny was ever seen. While studying at the Academy of Rome he could not have been more than twenty years old when he wagered six pads of grey paper with his fellows that he would climb alone to the top of the Coliseum.

160

e venturesome youth reached the ridge indeed,
ugh risking his life a score of times. When
attempted to descend, however, he was unable
use the jutting stones which had helped him
his ascent. It was found necessary to throw
rope to him from a window. He caught hold
it, bound it round his body, and sprang into
ice. Happily, his rescuers succeeded in getting
n into the interior of the monument. The
re account of this stunt makes one's hair stand
end. Robert is the only man who has ever
:ed attempt it. And just for six pads of grey
)er !

It was also he who got lost in the catacombs
Rome, and who was celebrated by the Abbé
lille in his poem " L'Imagination." Mme de
bllier, like ourselves, was aware of the adven-
e in the catacombs, and after hearing the
ses of the Abbé Delille, said : " The Abbé
lille has given me more pleasure, but Robert
ie me more fright."

The happiness which accompanied Robert
bughout his whole life seems to have been
h him even at his death. The good, merry
t did not foresee his end nor suffer the
uish of an agony. He was feeling very well
dressed ready to go out to dine. Mme Robert
just finished dressing, when she went to her
band's atelier to tell him she was ready, and
overed him dead, having had a lightning
plectic stroke.

THE DUCHESS DE POLIGNAC.

There is no slander, no horror which has been invented by hate and envy against Duchess de Polignac. So many libels have b written to damn her, that, together with vociferations of the revolutionaries, they m have left in the minds of some credulous peo the idea that the friend of Marie-Antoinette a monster. I knew that monster : she was finest, sweetest and loveliest woman one co wish to see.

A few years before the Revolution, the Duch de Polignac came to see me. I painted her port several times as well as that of her daughter, Duchess de Guiche. Mme de Polignac loo so young that she might have been taken { her daughter's sister. Both were the best-looki women of the Court. Mme de Guiche wou have made a perfect model for one of the Grac As for her mother, I will not attempt to descr her appearance. It was heavenly.

The Duchess de Polignac had besides her { lightful beauty an angelic sweetness and a m attractive, solid sense. All who were intimat acquainted with her have no difficulty in realiz why the Queen chose her for a friend, for she i indeed the Queen's friend. To this fact she ow her position as governess to the royal childr Her appointment immediately drew upon her ceaseless rage of all the women who coveted post. Hundreds of atrocious calumnies were fi

162

JOSEPH CAILLOT NÉ A PARIS

CAILLOT THE ACTOR.
By Voiriot.

To face p 163.

off against her. I often heard people of the
Court talking against her, and I confess that I
was revolted by such dark and persistent wickedness.
What no courtier could believe, though it was
the pure truth, was that Mme de Polignac had
not coveted the post she occupied. It is possible
her family were very glad to see her advanced to
the dignity, but she herself had only yielded out
of respect for the Queen's desire and at the constant
entreaties of the King. All that she longed to
have was her liberty. In fact, life at Court was
quite unsuited to her. Being indolent and lazy,
she would have found delight in rest, whereas
the duties of her post seemed to her like a heavy
burden. Once when I was painting her profile
at Versailles, hardly five minutes went by without
our door being opened and people inquiring
about her orders and scores of things concerning
the children. " Well ! " she said to me at last,
with a look of utter boredom, " every morning
it is the same questions. I never have a moment
to myself till dinner-time, while other fatigues
await me in the evening."

At the Château de la Muette, where she spent
the summer, she was able to enjoy a little more
freedom. The royal children were very happy
here, and she used to give small informal balls,
which were very amusing. It was there that she
gave birth to Count Melchior de Polignac, at
the same time her daughter gave birth to the
present Duke de Guiche.

Shortly before the Revolution she begged the

King to accept her resignation, which he refuse
to do. Being obliged, however, to take care o
her health, she obtained permission to take th
baths at a famous watering-place in England
She set out with the firm intention of giving u
her post on her return ; but I know for certai
that the King, fearing lest her resignation migh
grieve the Queen, went down on his knees t
beg her to remain the governess of the roya
children. It is easy to realize how the manifesta
tion of favour so dazzling and abiding arouse
the fury of the envious. Hatred of the favourit
grew yet stronger. It vastly helped the approaching Revolution, which was soon to strike botl
the Polignacs and their enemies.

THE PRINCE DE LIGNE.

I made the acquaintance of the Prince de Lign(
at Brussels. When he came to France shortl
before the Revolution, we renewed our acquaintanc(
with so much pleasure that he spent a good numbe
of his evenings at my house. When he, the Abb'
Delille, the Marquis de Chastellux, Count d.
Vaudreuil, Vicomte de Ségur, and several othei
of those days, were gathered together round m'
fire, the conversation was so lively and interestin;
that we found it very hard to break up the party

Mme de Staël referred to the Prince de Ligne i
the following manner : " He is perhaps the onl
foreigner who ever became a model of the Frenc
manner instead of being an imitator ! " Elsewhei
she said : " The Prince de Ligne saw men, thing

THE PRINCE DE LIGNE.
After A. Bartsch (1789).

To face p. 165.

and events pass before his eyes. He judged them without trying to impose upon them the tyranny of a system. He knew how to put sense into everything ! ''

The sense of which Mme de Staël was so good a judge, having so much herself, was one of the chief charms of the Prince de Ligne. His brilliant imagination, subtle comments on all subjects, and witty remarks, which were constantly running all over Europe, were never able to rouse in the Prince de Ligne any desire to be listened to. His speech and manners remained so unaffected that a fool might have taken him for an ordinary man.

He was tall and had a very noble bearing, without staidness or affectation. The charm of his mind was so well expressed in his face that I have known few men whose first appearance was so prepossessing, while his good nature soon captured your affection. He was both a brave and learned soldier. His profound knowledge of warfare has been appreciated throughout Europe, while the love of glory had always held its sway over him. On the other hand, his indifference to money was excessive. Not only did his extreme generosity involve him in enormous expenses, which he always refused to reckon up, but when I saw him again in Vienna in 1792 he came to the house of Mme de Rombech one evening in order to tell us that the French had taken possession of all his property in Flanders, and he seemed to take the news very little to heart. " I have only two louis left," he added with a detached look. ' Who is going to pay my debts ? ''

The only loss that affected him deeply wa that of his son Charles. This brave young mai died gloriously at the battle of Boux, in Champagne The blow which struck him, struck the Prince d Ligne as well. It deprived him for ever of hi gaiety and all pleasure in life.

Everybody knows the *Memoirs and Letters o the Prince de Ligne,* whose style—*le style parlĕ* as Mme de Staël calls it—has a charm of its own The letters I prefer are those he addressed to th Marquise de Coicelles during his travels in th Crimea with the Empress Catherine, of which h often talked to us. The letters bring him to lif again to me, especially the letter he wrote fron Parthenizza. It is so full of witty and philo sophical ideas, and reveals the mind and soul o the Prince so well, that it appears to me like moral prism. I have read the letter a dozei times, and I hope to read it again.

COUNTESS D'HOUDETOT.

I made the acquaintance of Countess d'Houdeto long before the Revolution. She was then th centre of all the celebrated wits and artists o Paris. As I desired very much to see her, m friend, Mme de Verdun, who was intimatel acquainted with her, took me to Sannois, wher Mme d'Houdetot had a house, and got me invite for the day. I knew she was not good-looking but remembering the passion with which she ha inspired J. J. Rousseau, I expected at least t find she had a pleasant face. I was so very mucl

166

MADAME DUGAZON.

To face p. 16

disappointed at finding her so ugly that her romance vanished from my imagination on the spot. She was so boss-eyed that when she spoke to you it was impossible to make out whether her words were meant for you. At dinner I thought every time she offered me a dish that she was offering it to somebody else, so equivocal was her gaze. It must be said, however, that her sweet nature made one forget her ugliness. She was kind and indulgent, and rightly beloved of all those who knew her. As I always considered her worthy to inspire the tenderest sentiments, I came to believe after all that she was able to inspire a man with love.

The Maréchal de Biron. The Maréchal de Brissac.

The face, figure and appearance of these two old bulwarks of the French monarchy have remained so well impressed on my mind that I should be quite capable of painting them from memory at the present day.

Having heard about the fine garden attached to the Biron mansion, which was said to be full of the rarest flowers, I sent a request to the Maréchal for permission to visit it. This I received, and accordingly I went there with my brother one morning. In spite of his great age (eighty-four, I believe) and his infirmities, the Maréchal Biron came out to meet me, though he walked with difficulty. He came down the steps of his broad terrace in order to give me his hand when I alighted from my carriage, and then excused himself for not being able to show me round his garden. After my walk round the garden I returned to the salon, where he kept me a long while. He talked with elegance and ease, referring to old times in a way that interested me immensely. When I went back to my carriage, he insisted on giving me his arm as far as the bottom of the terrace steps, and with bare head and body erect waited until he had seen me leave before entering the house. This gallantry in a man past eighty seemed to me most charming.

He died in 1788. He was spared the pain of witnessing the defection of the Gardes Françaises. He had tightened up the discipline in that body so rigorously that his successor, the Duke du Châtelet, slackened it beyond measure just before the Revolution arrived.

Regarding the Maréchal de Brissac, I only saw him at the Tuileries, where he was fond of walking about. He looked very old, but held himself very upright and walked like a young man. His costume attracted attention, for he always wore his hair in plaits, which formed two pigtails at the back of the head, while his coat was long and flowing with a girdle below the waist and gold-edged stockings rolled about his knees. This ancient costume did not make him at all grotesque. He looked extremely noble, and seemed like a courtier coming out of the halls of Louis XIV.

M. DE TALLEYRAND.

One morning Chamfort brought to my house
M. de Talleyrand, who was then Abbot of Péri-
gord. His features were gentle, his cheeks very
round. Though lame, he was none the less
elegant, and said to be well-off. He said very
little to me beyond a few remarks on my pictures.
I had my reasons then for believing that he merely
wished to find out whether I lived in the midst
of as much luxury and grandeur as I was said to
do, and that Chamfort brought him in order to
prove the contrary. My bedroom, which was
the only room in which I could receive him,
was furnished in the simplest manner, as M. de
Talleyrand and many other persons may remember
at the present day.

I don't think he ever came to my house again,
but I saw him a while at Gennevilliers, when he
came to dine with Count de Vaudreuil. I also
saw him later, on my return to France. He was
then married to Mme Grant, a very good-looking
woman whose portrait I had painted before the
Revolution. A rather amusing story is told about
her : M. de Talleyrand, having invited Denon
to dinner on his return from accompanying Bonaparte in Egypt, urged his wife to read a few
pages of the celebrated traveller's history, so that
she might be able to say something pleasant to
him. He added that she would find the volume
in his writing-table. Mme de Talleyrand obeyed,
but made a mistake and read a fairly large part

of the adventures of Robinson Crusoe. At table
she put on her most charming look and said to
Denon : " Ah ! Monsieur, I have just read your
book with the utmost delight ! How interesting
it is, especially when you describe how you met
that poor Friday ! " Heaven knows what Denon
looked like at these words, and above all M. de
Talleyrand ! This little story went all round
Europe. Perhaps it is not true. It is certain, however, that Mme de Talleyrand had a very poor wit
In this respect her husband had enough for two.

DOCTOR FRANKLIN.

I first saw Doctor Franklin when I was painting
the portrait of Monsieur, afterwards Louis XVIII
He had come with the other ambassadors to make
his visit to the Court. I was struck by his extreme
simplicity. He wore a plain grey coat and flat
unpowdered hair reaching to his shoulders. But
for his noble face, I should have taken him for
a big farmer, so great was his contrast with the
other diplomats, who were all powdered, in full
dress, and splashed all over with gold and ribbons
No man in Paris was more lionized than
Franklin. Crowds ran after him in the promenades and public places. Hats, sticks, snuff
boxes, everything was named after him, and i
was considered a great honour to be invited to
dinner at which that celebrated personage was
present. I may say, however, that meeting him
even very frequently, was not enough to satisf
the curiosity he aroused. I often saw him at the
170

FRANKLIN.

By Houdon (Musée de Versailles).

To face p. 170.

house of Mme Brion, who lived at Passy. Franklin spent all his evenings there. Mme Brion and her two daughters provided music which he seemed to listen to with pleasure, but during the intervals, I never once heard him speak so much as a word, and I was tempted to believe that he was vowed to silence.

THE PRINCE OF NASSAU.

I was still unmarried when the young Prince of Nassau was presented to me by the Abbé Giroux. He asked me to paint his portrait, which I made full length, of a small size, in oils. The Prince of Nassau, called " the Invulnerable " by the Prince de Ligne, had already gained a reputation for his dazzling deeds of heroism that seemed almost fabulous. His whole life was a series of surprising adventures. He was hardly twenty when he went with Bougainville on a journey round the world, and penetrated into the deserts, where his daring earned for him the name of the Monster-tamer. Since then he has fought victoriously on land and sea against all the nations of the world. Always at it, warring or otherwise, he has been all over the world from one end to the other. Hence it was said that his letters should be addressed to him on the great roads.

There was nothing in the face and appearance of the Prince of Nassau to indicate the hero of so many adventures. He was tall and well-made, while his features were regular and fresh-complexioned. But the extreme gentleness and

171

habitual repose of his looks gave no hint of th
great deeds and intrepid valour which marke
him out among all others. I met him again a
Vienna during the emigration. I had taken m
daughter, who was then about nine years old, t
the house of Casanova. The latter had painte
several pictures of the Prince de Nassau in th
act of felling lions and tigers. Shortly after, w
were visiting the Princess de Lorraine one evening
when the Prince de Nassau was announced. Ex
pecting to see a ferocious individual, my daughte
whispered to me : " Oh ! is that the man
heard so much about ? He looks as gentle an
shy as a girl just out of the convent."

M. DE LA FAYETTE.

Shortly before the Revolution, I was paid
visit by M. de La Fayette. He merely came t
see the portrait I was painting of pretty Mme d
Simiane, whom he was said to be looking afte
I never met him again. We should find it rathe
hard to recognize each other, for I was young a
the time of his visit, as he was too, though it wa
after his journey to America. He seemed t
have a pleasant face. His tone and manner wer
very well bred and gave no sign whatever of hi
revolutionary inclinations.

MADAME DE LA REYNIÈRE.

After my marriage I sometimes went to suppe
with Mme de La Reynière and to the evening
parties she used to give in the house which he
172

CAILLOT, THE ACTOR, AS TOM JONES.

To face p 172

husband built in the Rue des Champs Elysées, where the best society in Paris met.

Mme de La Reynière's maiden name was Jarente. Her family were noble and very poor, and had made her marry M. (Grimod) de La Reynière, one of our wealthiest financiers. Everything about her showed the disgust she felt in having to be called by a bourgeois name. She was good-looking, very tall and very thin. Her noble and haughty air was remarkable. She established herself as reigning mistress of the house, where she always received her guests with the grandest dignity, in order to let no one forget who she was born. When Doyen the painter was asked one day after dining at her house what he thought of Mme de La Reynière, he replied : " She receives very well, but I believe she is suffering from nobility."

Her husband was a good fellow in every sense of the word, easy to get along with, and never speaking evil of anybody. Nevertheless he was turned into ridicule, or rather he was made fun of because he fancied he could paint and sing. He spent all his time exercising these two imaginary talents, one in the morning, the other in the evening. He had a perfect dread of thunder, power could have made him come out before the sky was all clear once more. As he maintained he was not afraid of thunder and only took refuge in the cellar in order to avoid the vivid impression made on his nerves by the storm somebody wantonly devised a means to deprive the poor man of his excuse. One day he went to play a game of cards at the château of the Duchess de Polignac at La Muette, where she used to spend the summer. The card-table was set before a window opening into the park. At the base of the window Count de Vaudreuil had placed a couple of squibs. M. de La Reynière was enjoying a quiet game, the weather being very calm, when of a sudden the squibs went off with a loud bang. He got such a terrible fright, crying out "Thunder! Thunder!" that he almost fell ill. His fears were soon removed when the thing was explained to him. It was proved, however, not that his nerves were affected by thunder, but that he was afraid of it.

Mme de La Reynière's society was made up of the most distinguished people of the Court and town. She also attracted to her house the outstanding personalities in the arts and literature The Abbé Barthélemy, author of *Anacharsis*, spent his life there. Witty and pleasant Count d'Adhémar went there almost every day, as did Count de Vaudreuil and Baron de Besenval, Colonel General of the Swiss Guards. Mme de La Reyniére's great evening receptions usually brought together the most fascinating women of the Court

MADAME DUGAZON AS NINA.
By Dutertre.

To face p 174.

It was there that I made the acquaintance of Countess de Ségur, who was then as good-looking as she was kind and nice. Her sweetness and affability were prepossessing. She never left her old and infirm father-in-law, the Maréchal de Ségur, who found in her a veritable Antigone. Her husband, who was noted for his wit and literary talent, was at that time Ambassador in Russia.

To complete the charm of Mme de La Reynière's receptions, music was often performed in the gallery by Sacchini, Piccini, Garat, Richer, and other celebrated artists. Indeed, it would be difficult to convey an adequate idea of the delights of those gatherings, of the amenity and good manners which prevailed in those salons among people delighted to be in one another's company. Moreover, at the time I am speaking of there were several houses of this kind. I will mention above all those of the wives of Maréchal de Boufflers and Maréchal de Luxembourg. Though it must be admitted these two great ladies were not considered to be the most moral women of their time, young women eagerly resorted to their houses. Some of them said to me: "It is there that we get the best lessons in the manners of good society and receive the best advice." The Marquise de Boufflers, daughter-in-law of the Maréchal and mother of the Chevalier de Boufflers so famous for his wit, was the author of a delightful song, a sort of social code, which I reproduce here because it is little known :

175

To the tune of " Sentir avec ardeur flamme discrète."
Il faut dire en deux mots ce qu'on veut dire,
Les longs propos sont sots.
Il faut savoir lire
Avant d'écrire,
Et puis dire en deux mots ce qu'on veut dire.
Les longs propos sont sots.
Il ne faut pas toujours parler,
Citer,
Dater,
Mais écouter ;
Il faut savoir trancher l'emploi
Du moi, du moi,
Voici pourquoi :
Il est tyrannique,
Trop académique;
L'ennui, l'ennui
Marche avec lui.
Je me conduis toujours ainsi
Ici ;
Aussi
J'ai réussi.[1]

Coming back to the subject of Mme de La Reynière, it may be noted that when she became a widow she was left with a son who was far from sharing his mother's pride of nobility, and must have exasperated her many a time on that score. First of all, he persisted in calling himself Grimod de La Reynière (M. de La Reynière's original

[1] " One should say in a couple of words what one has to say. Long-winded talk is stupid. One must know how to read before writing, and then say in a couple of words what one has to say. Long-winded talk is stupid. One should not always talk, quote, date, but listen. One should know how to cut down the use of the personal pronoun, because it is a despot and too academic. Boredom is its companion. I always behave in this way here. Hence I have succeeded."

me was Grimod), and more often than not just
ain Grimod. Moreover, he was on affectionate
rms with his father's relations, and very often
his mother's grand dinners he would talk before
the Court of his uncle the grocer, or his cousin
e hairdresser, which put the poor woman on
nterhooks.

Young Grimod de La Reynière had plenty of
t, though he was fond of being original in all
rts of things. For instance, he would never
ear his hat. Having an amazing wealth of hair,
got his valet to do it up into an enormous
upet. Being in the amphitheatre of the Opéra
ie day, when a new ballet was being performed,
happened to sit in front of a small man who
irted to curse at the top of his voice this new
nd of wall that shut out his view of the stage.
red of seeing nothing, the little man began to
ike one of his fingers through the toupet, then
poked another finger through and so ended
making a sort of quizzing-glass to which he
it his eye. During all this procedure M. de
Reynière neither stirred nor uttered a word.
the end of the performance, however, he rose
d putting out one hand stopped the man who
is about to leave ; with the other hand he drew
ittle comb from his pocket, saying in the coolest
nner : " Monsieur, I let you do everything
u cared to my toupet in order to help you to
the ballet at your ease. But I am going out
supper and you must realize I cannot possibly
esent myself in the state to which you have

reduced my hair, so you will have the goodne to rearrange it, or to-morrow we shall cut eac other's throats."—" Monsieur," replied the littl man, laughing, " God forbid I should fight man who has been so kind to me as you. I wi do my best." And taking the comb, he dre the hair together somehow, after which the separated like the best friends in the world.

DAVID.

I was always eager for the society of all artis of note, especially of distinguished artists in m own art. David, therefore, came pretty often my house. Suddenly, however, he ceased comin Meeting him in society one day, I felt obliged reproach him gently on the subject. He replied " I don't like being in the company of Cou people."—" How ! " I exclaimed. " Could yo possibly have noticed that I treat Court peop better than others ? Have you not seen me we come everybody with the same regard ? " As persisted, I added laughingly : " Ah ! I belie you are proud and grieve at not being a du or marquis. For my part, I am utterly indiffere to titles and receive all nice people with pleasure

David never came to my house again aft that. He even extended to me the hatred bore to some of my friends. This is proved the fact that later on he got hold of some so of big book written against M. de Calonne, which were related all the odious calumnies again myself. He always kept this book in his atelie
178

P. A. CARON DE BEAUMARCHAIS

BEAUMARCHAIS.
By Cochin.

To face p. 179.

ing on a stool and open at the page where I
as discussed. Such a piece of malice was so
lack and puerile that I would never have believed
, had I not been told about it by M. de Fitz-James,
ount Louis de Narbonne and other acquaintances,
ho saw the thing on more than one occasion.
It must be said, however, that David was so
nd of his art that no amount of hatred prevented
m from doing justice to any talent one might
ve. After my departure from France I sent
Paris the portrait of Paesiello, which I had
ainted at Naples. It was hung at the Salon
791) beneath a portrait painted by David,
ith which the artist was doubtless not satisfied.
pproaching my picture, he looked at it a long
hile, then, turning to some of his pupils and
her persons standing around him, he said:
One would think my portrait was done by a
oman and Paesiello by a man." I was told
is by M. Le Brun, who was present at the time.
oreover, I am certain that David never refused
give me his praise.
It is quite likely that such flattering praises of
y talent might have induced me to forget David's
tacks on my person, but I have never been able
forgive his atrocious conduct during the Terror.
e indulged in cowardly persecutions of a great
mber of artists, especially Robert the landscape
inter, whom he had arrested and treated in
ison with barbarous severity. I should never
ve been able to meet such a man again. On
y return to France one of our most celebrated

painters (Gros) told me during a visit that David was very anxious to see me again. I made no reply, and as the painter in question had plenty of gumption, he realized that my silence was not of the kind referred to by the proverb : " Who says nothing, consents."

M. DE BEAUJON.

Having been asked by M. de Beaujon to paint his portrait for the hospital founded by him in the Faubourg du Roule, I went to the magnificent mansion which is now called L'Elysée-Bourbon, as the unfortunate millionaire was unable to come to my house. I found him alone, sitting in a big arm-chair on castors in the dining-room. His hands and legs were so much swollen that he was unable to use them. His dinner was nothing more than a sad dish of spinach. But a little farther away, in front of him, stood a table prepared for forty diners. The food served at that table was said to be exquisite and was prepared for some intimate women friends of M. de Beaujon and the persons they cared to invite. These ladies, who were all of good birth and society were nicknamed in the world " M. de Beaujon' cradle-rockers." They gave their orders in the house, had the whole of his mansion and horse at their disposal, and paid for these advantages with a few moments' conversation which they granted to the poor invalid, who was tired of living alone.

M. de Beaujon wished to make me stay for dinner. I refused, as I never dined away from

MADAME VIGÉE-LE BRUN.
By herself.

To face p 181.

.ome. But we agreed on the price and pose of .is portrait. He wished to be painted seated at writing-desk, to the middle of the legs, with ›oth hands. I was not slow to begin and to ːnish the work. When I was able to do without he model, I took the canvas home to finish some ›f the details. I took it into my head to put the ›lan of the hospital on the desk. When M. de ʒeaujon got to hear of it, he immediately sent iis manservant to beg me to obliterate the plan, .nd to deliver to me thirty louis as a compensation or the time I had employed. I had barely drawn he sketch, and naturally I refused to take the hirty louis. The manservant returned next day .nd insisted so much on behalf of his master, hat in order to get him to take the money back was obliged to obliterate the plan in his presence, hereby proving to him that it had not taken up nore than five minutes of my time.

While I was working on the portrait of M. de ʒeaujon I wished to look over his fine mansion, vhich was fabled to be very magnificent. No ›rivate person, indeed, lived in the midst of so nuch luxury. Everything was costly and ex-ʃuisite. The first salon was hung with striking ›ictures, not one of which was really worthy of ɪote, though proving how easy it is to deceive ɪmateurs, whatever price they may put upon their ɪcquisitions. The second was a music-room, con-ɪaining large and small pianos and all kinds of ɪnstruments. Other rooms, such as the boudoirs ɪnd studies, were furnished with the greatest elegance. The bathroom especially was delightful It had a bed and a bath draped, like the walls with fine flower-spangled muslin with a pink lining. I have never seen anything so pretty It must have been very nice to have a bath in that room. The first-floor apartments were furnished with similar care. In the middle of one room, adorned with columns, there stood an enormous gilt, flower-circled basket enclosing a bed in which no one had ever slept. All that side of the mansion overlooked the garden, which in view of its size might be called a park. It was laid out by a clever architect and adorned with a vast quantity of flowers and green trees.

It was impossible for me to look over this delightful dwelling without feeling pity for its wealthy owner and recalling an anecdote I had heard a few days before. An Englishman, being anxious to see all the sights of Paris, asked for M. de Beaujon's permission to inspect the mansion. When he came to the dining-room, he discovered the table laid out, just as I had done. Turning to the manservant who was showing him round he said : " Your master must keep a very fine table ? "—" Alas ! " replied the man, " my master never sits down to table. He dines off nothing but a dish of spinach." The Englishman then passed into the first salon. " Here at least is plenty to delight his eyes," he exclaimed, pointing to the pictures.—" Alas, Sir, my master is nearly blind."—" Ah ! " said the Englishman, as he entered the music-room, " he makes up for that

182

BOUTIN.
By Cochin.

To face p 183.

suppose, by listening to good music ? "—" Alas,
ir, my master has never heard any of the music
hat is played here. He goes to bed too early
n the hope of sleeping a few moments." The
nglishman then looked out at the beautiful
arden and said : " But at least your master
an enjoy his walks."—" Alas, Sir, he can't walk."
t this moment the persons invited to dinner
rived, among whom were several very pretty
omen. The Englishman remarked : " However,
ere is more than one beauty that can give him a
ew enjoyable moments." In reply to this remark,
he manservant merely sighed " Alas ! " twice
nstead of once, and made no further comment.

M. de Beaujon was very small and fat, with no looks
t all. M. de Calonne, whom I painted at the same
me, was a perfect contrast to him. When the Abbé
Arnault saw the two portraits side by side at my house,
he exclaimed : " Behold the spirit and the matter."

M. de Beaujon had been banker to the Court
under Louis —, and his financial operations had
always been so clever that before he grew old
he was already possessed of millions. It must be
said in his praise that he spent a good deal of his
fortune on good works. No unfortunate ever
appealed to him in vain, while the hospital of the
Faubourg du Roule still reminds the public of
his benefactions to mankind.

M. Boutin.

Another immensely wealthy financier, who was
as benevolent as M. de Beaujon, was M. Boutin,

for whom I cherished much friendship. He was
no longer young when I made his acquaintance.
He was small, lame, gay and witty, and so good-
natured and kind that one grew attached to him
as soon as one knew him a little closer. As he
was immensely wealthy, he frequently received
his numerous friends with great dignity, without
interfering in any way with his good works in
connection with the poor. M. de Boutin was a
perfect host, as I was often able to judge. He
told me he had instituted on my behalf a Thursday
dinner, at which all my intimate friends were
present : Brongniart, Robert and his wife, Lebrun
the poet, the Abbé Delille, Count de Vaudreuil,
who never missed attending whenever he was in
Paris on a Thursday, etc., etc. We were never
more than twelve at table, and these dinners were
so amusing that they made me break my word
never to dine away from home. They took place
in M. Boutin's charming house at the top of a
magnificent garden which he had called Tivoli.
In those days the Rue de Clichy had not yet
been built, so that when you happened to be
there among the beautiful trees and avenues you
might think you were out in the country. I
may even say that that beautiful dwelling seemed
to me rather too isolated. I should have been
afraid to go there in the evening, and I often
advised M. Boutin never to go home alone.

After my departure from France my brother
wrote to me that M. Boutin still went on with
his Thursday dinners, in memory of me ; that
184

was always toasted, as was also Count de Vaudreuil,
ho had likewise emigrated. Unfortunately for
im, M. Boutin was of the same way of thinking
s M. de Laborde, who wrote to me in Rome
us : "I am remaining in France. I am un-
armed. As I have never done harm to
nyone . . . !" Alas ! good, kind M. Boutin
kewise had never done harm to anyone. Never-
1eless, they both fell beneath the revolutionary
atchet, for both were rich and their riches were
oveted. I am at a loss to describe the grief I
elt on learning the news. M. de Boutin was
ne of the men I shall regret my whole life long.

The Government took possession of all his pro-
erty. His beautiful park was utterly destroyed,
xcept for a small part which was turned into a
ashionable promenade under the name of Tivoli,
vhere very fine fétes are said to have been
given, though I never saw one. It is easy to
ealize that on my return to France I had not the
ourage to go back to that unhappy spot.

M. DE SAINT-JAMES.

M. de Saint-James was Fermier-Général, very
vell-to-do and a true financier in the fullest sense
of the word. He was a middle-sized man, big
nd fat, with the kind of ruddy complexion that
ne sees on persons of fifty or so, when they are
n good health and happy. M. de Saint-James
kept a very opulent house. He lived in one of
he fine mansions on the Place Vendôme, and
gave very large and good dinners at which thirty

or forty persons at least were present. Havin
been unable to refuse an invitation to go ther
once, I very much regretted being neither
gourmande nor a sweet-tooth, for in both thes
respects I should have been utterly satisfied. Th
numerous company, however, did not strike me
as being nearly so nice as what was to be found
at the house of M. Boutin. M. de Saint-James
received his guests in a manner much more hearty
than elegant. After dinner the guests went into
a superb drawing-room fitted out entirely with
mirrors, which, however, did not help the many
persons present, who were unacquainted with one
another, to carry on conversation together with
the sort of confidence and intimacy that goes to
make up the charm of conversation.

Later on, when M. de Saint-James had arranged
his house and superb garden at Neuilly, which
was always called La Follie Saint-James, he
begged me to go there and dine with some of
my friends. It was a pleasant day. He showed
us round the fine park which had cost a fortune.
Among other expensive follies, he had constructed
an imitation mountain, the enormous stones of
which were no doubt brought from afar at great
expense and looked as though they were merely
hung up. I confess I crossed it very quick, as
those immense arches looked far from safe.

In this superb habitation M. de Saint-James
was fond of giving wonderful entertainments. I
went there once to see a comedy acted. So many
persons had been invited and walked about the

WATELET.
By Cochin.

To face p. 186.

garden before and after the show that it looked like a public promenade.

It may be supposed that the Revolution did not come in time enough to punish M. de Saint-James for having displayed so much magnificence, for I have never heard it said, either abroad or since my return to France, that he was guillotined. A natural death must have spared him the fearful fate of M. de Laborde and M. Boutin.

COUNTESS D'ANGIVILLER.

Mme d'Angiviller was what is called a fine wit. She had this reputation when she was still Mme Marchais. Her society was composed of all the men of letters, and even savants. Count d'Angiviller, who was often among her guests, fell in love with her and married her. She had so much influence over him that he never spoke in her presence, though he had plenty of wit, good taste and knowledge, which could be easily enjoyed whenever his wife was absent.

It is quite impossible for me to say whether Mme D'Angiviller was ugly or pretty, though I saw her plenty of times and was often put beside her. But she always concealed her face beneath a veil, which she never removed even for dinner. The veil covered, besides her face, an enormous bouquet of green branches, which she always carried at her side. I could never make out how she could shut herself up together with the bouquet without getting a headache. But later on, when I went into her bedroom, I was still

187

more surprised to find it adorned with rows of planks bearing all sorts of green trees that were never removed even at night.

Mme d'Angiviller was the acme of politeness, but so oddly given to paying compliments that people sometimes felt she made a mockery of politeness. One day M. d'Angiviller gave a dinner to some artists of the Academy, at which Vestier was present. Vestier was a very good portrait-painter and had just exhibited at the Salon a very fine family group that had aroused much attention. He must have been about fifty years old, and was thin, pale, and amazingly ugly. Wishing to say something flattering to him, Mme d'Angiviller exclaimed very loud : " Really, Monsieur, I find you have grown quite handsome." Poor Vestier went as red as a cockerel and looked right and left to see whether the words might not have been addressed to any other but himself, which made me burst into a fit of laughter.

It was at the house of Mme d'Angiviller that I first dined with the Marquis de Biévre, who became famous for his puns. I was unlucky, for on the day in question he did not make any. But I was told of a very good one which he had addressed to the Queen. Her Majesty having asked him for a pun, M. de Biévre bowed before her and noticed she was wearing green shoes. Whereupon he said at once : " Les désirs de Votre Majesté sont des ordres ; l'univers est à ses pieds."

188

THE BOULEVARDS BY THE PAGODA OF THE HÔTEL MONTMORENCY.

By Lallemand.

To face p. 188.

GINGUENÉ.

Ginguené was presented to me by the poet
ebrun as his intimate friend, so that he some-
mes came to my evening parties, though I did
ot like him in any way. I thought him dry and
ithout any charm or cheer. He was out of
lace in my society, while his works were as dis-
asteful to me as his conversation.

In 1789 he read to us an ode he had just
omposed for M. Necker. It might very well be
aken for the programme of 1793, for in it he
poke of victims and asserted that France could
ot be regenerated without bloodshed. Such
trocious opinions made me shudder. Count de
audreuil, who was present, said nothing, but we
exchanged glances and I saw quite well that he
realized the nature of the man as well as I.

Ginguené never left his friend Lebrun-Pindare.
Immediately after the death of the latter he paid
a visit to Mme Lebrun, who, by the by, had
been a cook, and asked her for Lebrun's manu-
scripts, as he wished to publish them. On going
through them in order to put them in order,
Ginguené was somewhat taken aback to find more
than a hundred epigrams against himself, some of
them quite atrocious. The publisher naturally
put them all aside. But I have always suspected
him of having taken his revenge by printing too
many weak and useless things in the works of
Lebrun, which detracts considerably from a collection that might otherwise be excellent.

It is well known that he threw himself heart
and soul into the Revolution, and constantly
expressed his regret that it had not been in his
power to vote the death of Louis XVI.

VIGÉE.

My brother was one of those men who are
born to be made much of in society. He had a
very good manner, having been about a good
deal in high society, plenty of wit and instruction.
He wrote very pretty verses with considerable
ease, and acted comedy better than a good number
of actors. He contributed a good deal to the
charm and gaiety of our gatherings. Perhaps the
eagerness with which people sought his company
was detrimental to his literary career, for we
used to take up much of his time. Nevertheless,
he still had enough in which to gain distinction
as a man of letters. Besides the course of literature
which he gave at the Athénée with great success,
in spite of his coming after a course just given by
La Harpe, Vigée left a volume of light verse
and several comedies in rhyme, two of which,
Les Aveux Difficiles and *L'Entrevue*, remained a
long time in the repertory of the Théâtre Français.
I am even surprised they are no longer given,
especially *L'Entrevue*, a charming little piece,
which was admirably acted by Mlle Contat and
Molé.

While still young, my brother married the
elder daughter of M. de Riviére, the Chargé
d'Affaires for Saxony. She was a charming woman,

Auteur ingénieux et séduisant Lecteur,
A son double talent tout miracle est possible ;
Son esprit est aimable et son cœur est sensible ;
Le lire est un plaisir, le connaître un bonheur.

Ernest Dangé.

ETIENNE VIGÉE.
By Rivière.

To face p. 190.

ull of virtues and talents, an excellent musician
nd gifted with so good a voice that she sang at
ny house with Mme Todi without exciting any
unfavourable comparison.

My brother and Mlle de Rivière had only
one child by their marriage, my niece, my beloved
niece, who has given me back a daughter, since,
alas ! I lost my own.

THE MARQUIS DE RIVIÈRE.

I cannot ever think of this fine man without
recalling the knights of old. Everything about
him was chivalrous. He faced death a hundred
times, even the most horrible death, with the
utmost courage, coolness and perseverance in order
to serve the Prince to whom he had consecrated
his life. His devotion sprang from no ambition
but from the truest friendship, the like of which
is rare even among ordinary persons. This affection of the Marquis de Riviére for Count d'Artois
dominated every other sentiment. It led him
into exile, poverty and prison ; yet he never
thought he was making too great a sacrifice for
its sake. " I have nothing left," he said to me
one day in London. Then, placing his hand on
the spot where the portrait of his beloved Prince
always lay over his heart, he added : " But I
will shed my last drop of blood for him. Perhaps
Fate has spared my life so often in order that I
may be of use to him. If that is so, I shall be
very glad to have escaped death so often."

It was on account of this praiseworthy desire

that M. de Riviére always undertook the most
important and often the most dangerous missions.
He knew no rest ; he did not seem to need it.
He would set out for Vienna, Berlin, Petersburg,
taking to the kings who still remained on their
thrones the requests of a king who had lost his.
He was on the road day and night without stop-
ping, sometimes without taking food, and carried
out his mission with so much disinterestedness and
cleverness that he gained the esteem and respect
of all the sovereigns and diplomats of Europe.
These oft-repeated journeys were not dangerous
apart from the extreme fatigue that they caused
him. On the other hand, how many times he
penetrated into France, where he ran the risk of
losing his head ! In his numerous journeys to
Paris during the Reign of Terror how many
times his zeal and activity must have made him
face death ! God seemed to protect him. Once
when about to land in Brittany he found the
coast bristling with soldiers. He jumped from
the boat into the sea at once, remaining under
water until the coast was clear and he could reach
the shore. He went in and out of Paris, sometimes disguised as a match-seller, sometimes in an
entirely different disguise of the same class. During
the daytime he hid in the house of a good fellow
who had once been in his service and was utterly
devoted to him. Night was his only time for
action, and then at the risk of deadly perils.
Often he was unable to evade his pursuers except
by jumping over deep ravines, swimming rivers,

ffering hunger and thirst, and having no rest.
hus he was always successful in escaping till the
d affair of Georges Cadoudal.

I remember that just before that fatal under-
king I met him in London at a house where
chegru was also present. Declaring me to be
excellent physiognomist, M. de Riviére came
to me and pointed to the French General,
ying : "Take stock of that man. Do you
ink he's to be trusted?" Of course, I was
together ignorant of what the matter was about,
t I looked at Pichegru and replied without
sitation : "He can be trusted. Sincerity seems
me enthroned on his brow." Pichegru, indeed,
as never a traitor. It is only too true that he
as the first to die of the victims of that unhappy
tempt. The fate of M. de Riviére was not so
rrible, though his imprisonment was long and
uel. He told me on my return to France that
e first dungeon into which he was thrust was
ll of stagnant water reaching as far as his ankles.
to this plight is added the idea of his never,
rhaps, seeing the world again, together with his
ief at being so far from his beloved Prince
d from all his friends, one can imagine what
must have suffered. It was during that time
misfortune that M. de Riviére reverted to piety,
d found in religion all the necessary strength to
ar so many sufferings and privations.

After being in prison several years, he was
owed out on his word of honour not to leave
ance, for Bonaparte himself knew what M. de

Riviére's word of honour was worth. In fact, h
kept it scrupulously, till the day he had th
ineffable joy of seeing the Bourbons return.

It is common knowledge that the King mad
him a Duke, that he was sent as Ambassador t
Constantinople, and that Charles X had chosei
him to be the tutor of the Duke of Bordeaux
when he died a premature death, to the grea
regret of his young pupil, his beloved Prince, and
one may say, of the whole of France.

Hearing that Charles X was deeply grieved a
the loss of such a friend, and having alread
painted the portraits of several persons fron
memory, I tried to paint that of M. de Riviér
as well. I was lucky enough to succeed. I a
once took the portrait to the King, who receive
it with great emotion, exclaiming with tears i
his eyes : " Ah ! Madame Le Brun, how gratefu
I am to you for your happy and touching idea !
I was more than paid by these words. Never
theless, the following day I received from Hi
Majesty a superb *nécessaire* in silver gilt, which
will keep all my life.

The Duke de Riviére was middle-sized, neithe
handsome nor ugly. All that could be notice
in his countenance was the extreme fineness c
his look, which, together with the expression c
sincerity and good-nature, indicated the whol
character of the man. Even as I depict hin
M. de Riviére always made the most brilliar
conquests. These were not due to his exteric
advantages, but to the qualities of his soul, whic

IN THE PARK.

After Moreau, junior.

To face p. 19

procured for him so many faithful friends. Among several distinguished beauties who had an affection for him, the last was undoubtedly the prettiest woman at the Court. She loved him as long as he lived, and M. de Riviére held her memory in great affection. He used to wear her portrait next his heart, beside the portrait of Count l'Artois. He showed it to me in London. He did not commit any indiscretion in doing so, for his liaison with this charming person was known to everybody. On his return to France, he married a woman who adored him and whose one happiness he became. He had thereby several children.

In addition to his noble and fine character, M. de Riviére had plenty of wit. Some of his letters might well be printed as models of style, while the timely word never failed him in conversation. One day, for instance, he was lunching in Petersburg with Suvaroff, who held him in great esteem and affection. The General pointed to him and said to the Russian officers: "Let's drink to the bravest!"—"To your health, Monsieur le Maréchal," replied M. de Riviére at once.

The life of the Duke de Riviére was written by the Chevalier de Chazet under the title of *Mémoires*. All the necessary documents were placed at his disposal so that there might be no question as to the truthfulness of the work, which makes interesting reading and does honour alike to the heart and literary talent of the author.

M. DE BUFFON.

In 1785 I went with my brother and Count de Vaudreuil to dine with the celebrated savant and writer, Buffon. He was already very old, dying shortly after, at the age of eighty-one. I was struck at first by the severity of his looks, but as soon as he started talking, he seemed to be transformed. His face brightened up to such an extent that, without exaggeration, genius glowed in his eyes. We left him in order to sit down at table, while he remained in the drawing-room, as he could no longer eat anything but vegetables. His son and pretty daughter acted as hosts at dinner, after which we returned to the drawing-room for coffee. When the conversation started, M. Buffon took the lead and seemed to enjoy spinning it out. He recited several fragments of his works, which were all the more charming owing to the warmth and expression in the great man's mode of speech. It was fairly late when we took our departure from him with much regret. He thrilled me so much that I envied his son and daughter-in-law for being able to see and hear him every day.

M. LE PELLETIER DE MORFONTAINE.

M. le Pelletier de Morfontaine, sometime Merchants' Provost in the reign of Louis XV, was witty, well-informed, good-natured and well-bred. Yet I have never known anybody subjected to so much ridicule.

196

THE HÔTEL MONTMORENCY AND THE GUARDS' DEPOT.

By Lallemand.

To face p.

He was very tall and thin. When I made his acquaintance he was about fifty-five years old and looked pale and faded. In order to brighten up his complexion, he used to smear a thick layer of rouge on his cheeks, and even on his nose. It was so obvious, that he declared his face would frighten people if he didn't paint it. This made his face already comic enough, and he surrounded it with so funny a head-dress that when I saw it for the first time I burst out laughing. It was a large Treasurer's wig, the toupet of which rose to a point like a sugar-loaf, while long curls fell down to the shoulders. It was powdered white all over. Moreover, M. le Pelletier suffered from somewhat embarrassing infirmities which were not due to his age but to the misfortunes of Nature. He was always obliged to keep scented pastilles in his mouth and to avoid speaking close to people. He bathed his feet several times a day, and even at night, and always wore two pairs of shoes with double soles. In spite of all these precautions it was impossible to sit near him in a closed vehicle. I underwent the sad experience with my sister-in-law in returning from Morfontaine. But, gracious me ! in spite of everything, M. le Pelletier was very forward with the ladies and thought himself to be in their eyes the most dangerous man of the world. He never ceased talking about his love affairs, successes and conquests, thereby giving rise to much fun.

The Chevalier de Coigny told me that on visiting M. le Pelletier one morning he discovered him stretched out on a pallet beside a table littered with phials, medicaments, satchells, etc., and so pale, not yet having painted his face, that M. de Coigny thought he was dying. "Ah! my dear Chevalier!" he said immediately, "how delighted I am to see you! You must give me your advice on a subject that gives me a good deal of concern. I must tell you that I have just broken off all my liaisons. I am free, absolutely free, and since you know the prettiest women of the Court, you are going to tell me which of them you advise me to pay my attentions to." The Chevalier de Coigny was perhaps the most amused of all of us at the funny ways of M. le Pelletier. Naturally he warmed to the occasion. He set about passing in review with him the women who were most remarkable for their beauty. But M. le Pelletier found in every one something that repelled him. This scene lasted a long while. "By heavens, man!" exclaimed at last the Chevalier, bursting into laughter. "Since you are so hard to please, I advise you to imitate handsome Narcissus and fall in love with yourself."

It was during M. le Pelletier's term of office as Provost that the bridge at the Place Louis XV was built. On that occasion the King gave him the Cordon Bleu, which was obtainable by virtue of office if a man did not belong to the high nobility. This ribbon turned his head to such an extent that he always wore it. I am tempted to believe that he wore it on his dressing-gown in the early morning. One day I caught sight of

198

ROUSSEAU'S TOMB AT ERMENONVILLE.

By Moreau, junior.

To   p. 199.

ıim climbing up the rocks that surround the
ake at Morfontaine. He was dressed as usual, as
hough he was· about to set out for Court. I
:alled out to him from below, where I was walking
ıbout deep in my rural day-dreams, that his
3lue Ribbon was utterly ridiculous in the midst
)f all that beautiful Nature. He never for a
noment felt any grudge against me for having
hus made him realize his oddity. For, after all,
t must be acknowledged that poor M. le Pelletier
was one of the best men that ever existed.

VOLTAIRE.

I was at the Comédie Française the day Voltaire
was present at the performance of his tragedy
Irene. In all my life I never saw such a triumph.
When the great man entered his box, the shouts
ınd clapping of hands were so great that I thought
he place would collapse. It was the same when
he crown was placed on his head. The celebrated
)ld man was so thin and frail that I feared such
.trong emotions would cause him mortal harm.
As for the piece, nobody listened to a word of
t. Nevertheless, Voltaire was able to leave the
beatre convinced that *Irene* was his best work.

I had a great desire to go and see him at the
ıouse of M. de Villette, with whom he was staying.
3ut I abandoned the idea, having heard that the
;reat number of visits he was being paid caused
ıim much fatigue. I can thus say that I only
went to his house in painting . . . in the following
nanner. Hall, the cleverest miniature painter of

199

the time, had just finished my portrait. It was a very good likeness and Hall showed it to Voltaire while on a visit. After looking at it for a long while, the celebrated old man kissed it several times. I confess I was greatly flattered at having received such a favour, and was very pleased with Hall for coming to tell me of it.

PRINCE HENRY OF PRUSSIA.

When Countess de Sabran presented me to the brother of the great Frederick, I set eyes on him for the first time. It is impossible for me to say how ugly I found him. He must have been aged about fifty years at the time, the King of Prussia being much older than he. He was small and slim, while his shape had no nobility, though he bore himself very upright. He had a strong German accent and gargled excessively. As for the ugliness of his face, it was at first sight utterly repulsive. Nevertheless, in spite of two large eyes, one looking right and the other looking left, his look had a certain gentleness, which was also noticeable in his voice. His speech was always full of great kindness, and in listening to him one grew accustomed to seeing him.

His military bravery is too well known to be talked about here. As the brother of Frederick, he was naturally fond of glory ; but it must be acknowledged that he was as responsive to a piece of human kindness as to a piece of heroism. He was good and set much store by the goodness of others.

He was passionately fond of the arts, especially music, and even took his first violin with him on his travels, so that he might cultivate his talent on the way.

His talent was rather middling, but he never missed a chance of exercising it. During his stay in Paris, he constantly came to my musical evenings. He was not at all afraid of the presence of the foremost virtuosi, and I never saw him refuse to take his part in a quartet beside Viotti, who played first violin.

COUNT D'ALBARET.

Another passionate amateur of music living in Paris at the same time was Count d'Albaret. Not only did he make it his business to attend all the concerts, but in spite of a small income he had his own body of musicians, after the manner of sovereigns. He boarded and lodged in his house nine or ten musicians, paying them a salary and allowing them to take pupils during their leisure hours.

These artists, as one may readily suppose, were all second rate. The singing lady, for instance, who sang only Italian airs, had a fairly good voice, but would never do for a prima donna, and I remember the singing master he gave me had a rather middling knowledge. The same could be said regarding his instrumentalists, not even excepting the first violinist. Nevertheless, all these people were so accustomed to team work and constant rehearsals that nowhere was such excellent music executed as at the house of Count d'Albaret. Hence, all music-lovers flocked to his concerts. These took place on Sunday morning. I went there several times, and always came away delighted.

COUNT D'ESPINCHAL.

Here you have a man whose business and pleasure, in a word, whose whole existence was confined to knowing, day by day, what was happening in Paris. Count d'Espinchal was always the first to be informed of a marriage, love intrigue, death, the reception or refusal of a play, etc.; so much so, that if anybody needed any information whatsoever about anybody or anything in the world, his or her first remark would be : " One must ask d'Espinchal about it." Of course, in order to be so well posted, he needed to know an amazing number of people. Hence he was unable to go down the street without greeting somebody at every step, ranging from the grand gentleman to the theatre boy, from the duchess to the charwoman and kept girl.

Furthermore, Count d'Espinchal went about everywhere. He was sure to be seen, if only for a moment, at the promenades, horse-races, in the salons, and in the evening at two or three shows. I could really never make out when he took his rest, for he spent almost every night at the balls.

At the Opéra and the Comédie Française, he knew exactly whom all the boxes belonged to. Most of them, it is true, were hired by the year

202

THE DUCHESSE D'ORLEANS.

By Madame Le Brun (Musée de Versailles).

To face p. 202.

n those days. He would have them opened one
after another in order to stay five minutes in each ;
or he had too much business in all directions to
pay long visits. He just spent time enough to
gather a few more bits of news.

Happily, Count d'Espinchal was not ill-natured,
otherwise he would have been able to upset many
a household, break off many liaisons of love or
friendship, and do harm to a good number of
persons. He was not even very talkative, and
knew how to hold his tongue with the persons
concerned in the numberless mysteries he managed
to discover. It was quite enough for his personal
satisfaction to be perfectly in the know regarding
all that was happening in Paris and at Versailles.
But to accomplish this aim he left no stone un-
turned, and was certainly better informed about
hundreds of matters than the Chief Constable
was.

Such a mania is so odd that in order to prove
its reality I will relate an incident that was known
by the whole of Paris at the time. One day, or
rather one night, Count d'Espinchal was at the
Opéra Ball. In those days the ball was not what
it has become nowadays ; it was frequented by
good society, and the best ladies of the Court
and town did not forego the pleasure of attending
it, " disguised to the very teeth," as the saying was.
For M. d'Espinchal, however, no disguise existed.
He recognized everybody at a glance. Hence
all the masked dominoes avoided him like the pest.
He was walking about the hall when he noticed

a man *he failed to recognize.* The man was running about, pale and scared, going up to all the
women disguised as blue dominoes and turning
aside in despair. The Count did not hesitate t
approach him, and said with a look of interest
" You appear to me to be in difficulties, Monsieur
If I can be of use to you by any means, I shall
be delighted."—" Ah ! monsieur," answered the
stranger, " I am the most miserable of men. Thi
morning I arrived from Orleans with my wife
who pestered me to take her to the Opéra Ball
I have just lost her in this crowd, and the poo
thing doesn't know the name of the hotel, no
even the name of the street where we have taker
lodgings."—" Put yourself at ease," replied th
Count. " I will lead you to her. Your wife i
sitting at the second window in the foyer." I
was indeed the lady. Overwhelmed with joy, he
stammered his thanks. " But how did you manage
to guess right, Sir ? "—" Nothing simpler,'
answered the Count. " Your wife is the only
woman at the ball whom I do not know, and .
had already concluded she must have arrive(
from the provinces quite recently."

When I returned to Paris under the Consulate
I saw Count d'Espinchal once again. " You mus
have lost your bearings altogether," I said t
him. " You no longer know anybody in the
boxes at the Opéra and the Comédie Française.'
His only reply was to raise his eyes to the ceiling
He died shortly after, of boredom no doubt, fo
he was not extremely old. Before dying, he i

THE LITTLE GODPARENTS.
After Moreau, junior.

To face p. 204.

id to have burnt an enormous quantity of notes
hich he was in the habit of jotting down every
vening. I had, indeed, been told about these
otes by several persons who, perhaps, were
raid of them. Certainly, they would have sup-
lied matter for a very piquant volume, and a
ery scandalous one into the bargain.

COUNTESS DE FLAHAUT.

Among the most distinguished women I knew
efore the Revolution I must not forget the
uthor of *Adèle de Sénange, Eugène de Rothelin,*
nd several other delightful works, which every-
ody has read at least once. Mme de Flahaut,
t the present day Mme de Souza, had not yet
ken to writing when I made her acquaintance.
Ier son, who is now a peer of France, was then
child of three or four. She herself was quite
oung. She had a pretty figure, a charming face,
he wittiest-looking eyes, and so much amiable-
ess that one of my pleasures was to spend the
vening at her house, where I usually found her
lone.
On my return to France I longed very much
o see her again. A vast amount of business and
arious occupations prevented me so long from
oing this that I no longer dared present myself
t her house. If by chance she reads these lines,
he will know that I am far from having forgotten
er.

MADEMOISELLE QUINAULT.

Mme de Verdun, one of my best friend acquainted me with Mlle Quinault, who had gaine celebrity as a great actress and was still famou as one of the wittiest and most learned women o her time. She had left the stage in 1741. Th intimate friend of M. d'Argenson and M. d'Alem bert, she presided over a salon which had becom the meeting-place of the most distinguished me of letters and society people in Paris. There wa much eagerness for the pleasure of spending few moments with her.

At the time of my acquaintanceship with he Mlle Quinault had, notwithstanding her great ag retained so much wit and mirth that she looke young to those who listened to her. Her memor was amazing. Certainly, she had had plenty o time to adorn it, for she was eighty-five year old. Among scores of anecdotes derived fror her remembrances, she told us how one day sh went to see Voltaire, with whom she was ver friendly, and discovered him in bed. He bega to talk to her about one of his tragedies, in whic he wished Lekain to wear a scarf, placed in particular way. In the heat of his descriptio Voltaire suddenly threw off the bed-clothes an pulled up his shirt in order to demonstrate scarf with it, leaving his decrepit body full exposed to the eyes of Mlle Quinault, who wa quite put out of countenance.

Mlle Quinault died, more than ninety year

MADEMOISELLE LE BRUN.

By the Comte de Chavoy.

To face p. 206

f age, in 1783. Mme de Verdun, who went
o see her one morning, was surprised to
nd her fully dressed and decked out with
ink ribbons, but in bed. " How ? " said
Mme de Verdun. " I have never seen you so
oquettish ! "—" I have dressed myself in this
vay," replied Mlle Quinault, " because I feel
am going to die to-day." The same evening
he passed away.

COUNT DE RIVAROL.

One morning my brother brought to see me
Count de Rivarol, who was very popular in the
most brilliant circles of Paris on account of his
wit, even before he had written anything. As I
was not expecting him, I was in my atelier putting
the finishing touches to several portraits I had
just painted. It is common knowledge that this
final work does not allow of any distraction, so
that in spite of the desire I had always felt to hear
M. de Rivarol talk, I was too much preoccupied
to enjoy all the charm of his conversation. Moreover, he talked so volubly that I was almost stunned.
However, I noticed that he had a handsome face
and an extremely elegant figure. None the less,
he must have thought me so clumsy that he never
came to see me again. Maybe some other reason
kept him from coming. He spent his life with
the Marquis de Champcenetz, who was always
very ill-natured towards me. Though possessing
neither the talent nor the brains of the author of

*Discours sur l'universalité de la langue Fran-
çaise*, the Marquis de Champcenetz had plenty of
wit, and generally used it to tear his neighbour to
shreds. Like M. de Biévre, he was fond of puns
and always making them, so that Rivarol called
him the epigram of the French language.

It was the Marquis de Champcenetz who, on
being condemned to death by the revolutionary
tribunal, gaily asked his judges whether he was
allowed to find a substitute as for service in the
National Guards.

PAUL JONES.

I often went to supper at the house of Mme
Thilorié, sister to Mme de Bonneuil, with that
celebrated sailor who rendered so many services
to the American cause and did so much harm to
the English.

His reputation had preceded him in Paris,
where everyone knew the number of battles in
which he had triumphed with his little squadron
over the ten times superior forces of England.
Nevertheless I have never met so modest a man.
It was impossible to get him to talk about
his great deeds, but on all other subjects he
willingly talked with a great amount of sense
and wit.

Paul Jones was a Scotsman by birth. I believe
he would have very much liked to become an
admiral of the French Fleet. I even heard that
when he returned to Paris a second time he made

request of this nature to Louis XV, who gave
im a refusal.

However that may have been, he went first of
ll to Russia, where Count de Ségur presented
im to the Empress Catherine II, who received
im with the utmost distinction and invited him
 dinner. He left Petersburg to join Suvaroff
nd the Prince of Nassau, with whom he dis-
nguished himself once more in the war against
e Turks. Back in Paris, he died during the
evolution, but before the Reign of Terror.

MESMER.

Having heard endless talk about this notorious
harlatan, I had the curiosity to assist once at
vhat he called his séances, in order to judge of
his jugglery for myself. On entering the first
oom, in which the adepts of animal magnetism
vere gathered, I saw a lot of people standing
ound a large, well-tarred tub. Most of the men
nd women held one another's hands to form a
hain. I wished at first to join in the circle, but
 thought I noticed that the man who was to
e my neighbour was mangy. You can imagine
ow quick I withdrew my hand and passed into
he next room. As I crossed the room accomplices
f Mesmer pointed small iron wands at me from
ll sides, which annoyed me amazingly. After
isiting the various rooms, all of which were full
f the sick and the inquisitive, I was about to go
way when I saw a tall, young, rather pretty girl

coming out of a neighbouring room, while Mesme held her hand. She was all dishevelled and de lirious, taking great care, however, to keep he eyes shut. A crowd gathered about them imme diately. " She is inspired," said Mesmer. " Sh can guess everything, though she is quite asleep. Then he made her sit down, seated himself i front of her and, taking her by both hands, aske her what o'clock it was. I noticed quite wel that he kept his feet on the feet of the pretende soothsayer, which made it quite easy to tell th time and even the minutes. Hence the girl' answers were so exact that she proved to be i agreement with all the watches of the assistants.

I confess I came away indignant at the idea c its being possible for such quackery to succee among us. Mesmer earnt heaps of money. N only did he gain immense profits from his muc frequented séances, but his numerous dupes ma a subscription for him, which, I was told, amounte to nearly five hundred thousand francs. He w soon obliged, however, to go to an unknow place in order to enjoy the fortune he had acquire in Paris. The rumour having got abroad th many indecent things were taking place at séances, the doctrines of this juggler were examine by the Academy of Science and the Royal Societ of Medicine, and the judgment of these t learned bodies regarding animal magnetism was such a nature that it obliged Mesmer to lea France.

Nowadays, when tubs and small iron wan

THE PRINCESS-ROYAL AND THE DAUPHIN.
By Madame Le Brun.

To face p 210.

have disappeared, we still find people who are
convinced that some woman or other, often quite
illiterate, sent to sleep by a magnetizer, can not
only tell you the time, but also guess your disease
and tell you the best treatment to follow. May
these sleep-walking sibyls do a lot of good to those
who consult them ! For my part, if I was ill, I
would rather call in a clever, wide-awake doctor.

M. Charles and M. Robert.

I saw the ascent in a balloon of the first two
men who had the courage to venture into the air
in so frail a contrivance, which had just been
invented by Montgolfier. They were Charles and
Robert. They had fixed their balloon to the
great basin at the Tuileries. On the day appointed
for the ascent (December 1, 1785) the garden
was filled with an enormous crowd, the like of
which I have never seen. When the ropes were
cut and the balloon rose majestically to so great
an altitude that it was lost to our sight, the admiration and fear for the two brave men in the
little basket drew a cry from every breast. Many
people—and I confess I was of their number—
had tears in their eyes. Happily, it was reported
a few hours later that Charles and Robert had
landed safely a few miles from Paris at a village
where the arrival of these passengers of the air
must have created quite a lively sensation.

M. Charles was a member of the Academy of
Science, and one of our most distinguished savants.

He was, moreover, an excellent man, being
sionately fond of music. Every year in
splendid laboratory he gave a series of lec
which were much frequented both by studen
science and people of society.

CPSIA information can be obtained
at www.ICGtesting.com
Printed in the USA
BVOW06s2143070717
488777BV00015B/244/P